Belgiculture!

(A Complete Master Plan for Solving the Countless Problems of Mankind!)

By
The Worldwide People's Revolution!®

Belgique Book 124 ♥ ♦

(The Cover Photo shows an Old Fortress with a Moat around it, which was the Best that they could Do with what they had to Work with, at that Time; but, now we have Far-Advanced Technologies to Work with!)

Copyright, Dedication and Introduction

By our Selected King's Chief Editor — Dr. Samuel Walker Edison — Ph.D., M.A., BS and QC!

ISBN — 979-8667-7229-15

00-01 [_] This Unique Book is COPYRIGHTED ADR 2020 by **The Worldwide People's Revolution!®** All Rights are Reserved for the Truth's Sake. No Portion of this Inspired Book shall be Reproduced by any Means for Sale without the Written Permission of "The Worldwide People's Revolution!" (A Comprehensive Plan for Obtaining Worldwide Law, Order, Obedience, Peace and True Prosperity!) By The Worldwide People's Revolution!® Book 108.

00-02 [_] The Readers might be Wondering WHY it is called BELGICULTURE? Well, that is beCause Belgium was the First Wise Nation to Recognize the Importance of "The GREAT Worldwide TELEVISED Court HEARING!" (That Great Meeting of the Most-Intelligent and Well-Educated Minds!) By The Worldwide People's Revolution!® Book 041B, which is Required for Solving the Countless

Problems of Mankind. beCause, only Provable Truths have the Power to Liberate us from the Prison of Lies, and only when the Masses of Intelligent People get to Hear those Provable Truths, whereby they might Judge the Value of them, and no longer be Walking in the Darkness of Ignorance; but, in the Bright Shining Light of PROVABLE TRUTHS!

00-03 [_] The Purpose for this Inspired Book is to SIMPLIFY the overall Master Plan of the Master Farmer for the Salvation of Mankind from our Massive Problems, without getting Bogged Down in Religious nor Political Details, which have filled Countless Volumes of many uninspired books, which do not even Capitalize Love nor Hate, in spite of the Fact that both are Equally as Necessary as Water and Fire, just to make Things Function Correctly. However, if the Burning Sunlight should get too Strong, all of the Ice in the Whole World could MELT, and all of Mankind would be in Double Trouble, you might say; but, it is more like Insurmountable Troubles without the Construction of those **"GLORIOUS Swanky Hotels Castles and Fortresses!" (Beautiful Planned City States for WISE Intelligent Well-Educated People with Common Sense and Good Understanding!) By The Worldwide People's Revolution!®** Book 019B, which will Solve no less than 5,000 of our Problems, if we have the Faith to Build them: beCause, they are "The Right Design for Living!" (A List of Great Advantages for Building Beautiful Planned City States!) By The Worldwide People's Revolution!® Book 012B, even if the Lady Doubtfulness does not Believe it, who must have Sea Water a Meter Deep in her own Kitchen, Living Room, and Bedroom, before she will even Consider it: beCause she is so Slow to Learn! ‡

00-04 [_] O Doctor Samuel Walker Edison, I Know Exactly what you Mean by that Lady Doubtfulness: beCause, I just Happen to have one of them Living within my own House, who Denies Climate Changes, who Sincerely Believes a Misinterpretation of the *Holy Bible,* which barely Mentions anything that is going on, Nowadays, and absolutely nothing in the Way of "Guaranteed Solutions!" (HOW to Solve our Local and Global Problems in the Most-Rational Manner Possible!) By The Worldwide People's Revolution!® Book 080, which is very Sad: beCause so many People Rely on those Jewish Fables to Save them from their Troubles.

00-05 [_] Well, my Friend, this Inspired Book is now DEDICATED to all such Stubborn People.

00-06 [_] O Doctor Sam, does the Selected King of "The Worldwide People's Revolution!" (A Comprehensive Plan for Obtaining Worldwide Law, Order, Obedience, Peace and True Prosperity!) By The Worldwide People's Revolution!® Book 108, actually have Guaranteed Solutions for ALL of our Massive Problems? For Example, HOW would he have us PREVENT all of the Millions of Vehicular Accidents and hundreds of thousands of Deaths in this World? †§‡

00-07 |_| Well, my Friend, the Wise People, who Liv within those **"GLORIOUS Swanky Hotels Castles and Fortresses!"** use Elevators, Escalators, and Electric Subway Trains, which are Powered by the WIND and WATER, which will Solve no less than 1,000 Problems, including Traffic Tickets, Traffic Jams, Noisy Sirens, Bloody Accidents, Car Insurance, Drive-by Shootings, Icy Highways to Drive on, Slippery Sidewalks, Greasy Filthy Streets, Children getting Run Over on Streets while Playing Ball Games, Pets getting Run Over, Wasted Gas at Stop Lights, Pollution from Vehicles, Lung Diseases, Doctor Bills, Hospital Bills, Drug Bills, and every Evil Thing that is Related with those DANGEROUS Vehicles, which are Totally Unnecessary for True Prosperity.

00-08 [_] So, O Doctor Sam, is our Selected King a Self-Appointed SAVIOR of Mankind; or, will we get to "VOTE for The GOAT!" (The New Political Party that has Guaranteed Solutions for our Massive Problems!) By The Worldwide People's Revolution!® Book 109? After all, it Sounds as if "All of the Arguments are in Favor of our Selected King, who has Zero Challengers!" (Before you Attend another Election Deception, you should Carefully Study this Inspired Book with an Honest Open Mind!) By The Worldwide People's Revolution!® Book 085. Indeed, there are no less than **"101 Good Reasons and Great Advantages for Establishing a Righteous One-World Government!"** (Government By the People, Of the People, and For the People!) By The Worldwide People's Revolution!® Book 104, which is very Good News, I would say, which is WHY that I am going to Check the above Box [_] and that Box with a LARGE GREEN-X MARK: beCause, I Agree with the Statement. However, if I Disagreed with that Statement, I would Check it with a LARGE RED-X MARK: beCause, there are Bound to be some Statements within this Inspired Book that I will STRONGLY Disagree with!

00-09 [_] Well, my Friend, before you Check any Boxes with any Marks of any Colors, I Strongly Suggest that you Carefully REED the entire Book, FIRST, whereby you might make Better Decisions the Second Time that you Reed it: beCause there are many Sarcastic Statements within this Inspired Book, which are Good for making People THINK, even though most People do not Like to Think: beCause it is Extremely Painful for them to Do so. Indeed, they Prefer to DREAM.

> A-[_] O Doctor Sam, I Agree with you — Thinking is very Painful when that Part of your Brains is Malfunctioning, as in

the Cases of Multitudes of Ignorant Americans, who have Suffered with House Fires for Centuries, and yet they Still Build those almost Worthless Wooden / Plastic Firetrap Mouse-infested Cockroach Dens, instead of Building those "Beautiful Swanky Stone Dome Home COMPLEXES!" (HOW to Build SECURE Tax-proof, Insurance-proof, Self-air-conditioned, Paint-proof, Rot-proof, Termite-proof, Mouse-proof, Fireproof, Tornado-proof, Hurricane-proof, Thief-proof, and BOMB-PROOF Houses!) By The Worldwide People's Revolution!® Book 102. †§‡§§

B-[_] I Sincerely Believe that only a Handful of Rich People could ever Afford to Build any such SECURE Houses for themselves to Liv in: beCause, just one of those Complexes might Cost a BILLION Dollars! Therefore, I am going to Check the above Box with a LARGE GREEN-X Mark, and Pray to God that I am not brought to Court to Prove it! §‡

C-[_] And why in the World would you be Afraid to be brought to COURT to Prove a simple Thing like that — seeing that "The New RIGHTEOUS One-World Government!" (HOW to Establish a Righteous One-World Government without Going to WAR!) By The Worldwide People's Revolution!® Book 056, has an Unlimited Supply of GOOD MONEY, which must be Earned by Honest Labor during the Construction of those "GLORIOUS Swanky Hotels Castles and Fortresses!"

— which will Represent that New Money, which will make it the Best Money in all Christendom? ‡

D-[_] Damned if I know what "Christendom" is; nor do I Care to Learn what it is: beCause I am a True Christian, who was Born Again, Physiologically, after Fasting with Jesus and Saint Paul for 40 Days and 40 Consecutive Nights on Mount Sinai with Moses and Elijah! See *Deuteronomy 9:9, 18; Second Kings 17; Matthew 4;* and *Second Corinthians 11:27.*§§

E-[_] Educated People do not Do any Fasting nor Praying: beCause they are Filled with the Holy GHOST, who Impregnated Mother Mary with the Baby Jesus, which was a Holy Act of Royal Fornication, you might say: beCause one of the Gods got Horny with Lusts.§

F-[_] I Fail to Understand what this Survey of my Values is all about? Why not just get on with the Belgiculture Beliefs, whereby we Education Slaves, Work Slaves, Tax Slaves, Insurance Slaves, Rent Slaves, Home-owner Slaves, Interest Slaves, Mortgage Bills Slaves, ElecTrickery Bills Slaves, Food Bills Slaves, Water Bills Slaves, Gas Bills Slaves, Transportation Bills Slaves, Repair Bills Slaves, Telephone Bills Slaves, Internet Bills Slaves, Entertainment Bills Slaves, Drug Bills Slaves, Doctor Bills Slaves, Hospital Bills Slaves, Childcare Bills Slaves, Nursing Home Bills Slaves, and Funeral Home Bills Slaves might be Set FREE with the First Church of Jesus Christ, who had NO BILLS nor Pills, at all? Yes, it is all Explained in: **"The New MAGNIFIED Version of the Book of ACTS!" (The Understandable Version of the Acts of the Apostles in Plain English!) By The Worldwide People's Revolution!®** Book 063, which any 12-year-old Child could Reed.

G-[_] God Knows that no 12-year-old Child could Afford to Buy such a Good Book, whereby he or she might Discover HOW that we have all been made into **"Modern Deceived SLAVES!" (10 Simple Steps for Liberating ALL Modern Slaves, Worldwide, Including Yourself!) By Liberty and Justice for ALL!** Book 113; but, their Parents might be able to Afford to Buy such an Enlightening Book, if they Learned that it was GOD who Wrote it! After all, it is a Near-Perfect Book, much like this Inspired Book; but, only AFTER you get about

20 to 30 pages into it: beCause that is the Way that God Inspires his Servants to Write his Inspired Books, which is just the Nature of such Things.

H-[_] HALLELUIAH! It looks like God has come Alive, once again! Where has he been Hiding himself for the past 2,000 or so Years? Is this for Real? Is the Kingdom of Heaven finally Coming to this War-torn World? Will Jesus Christ be Coming on his White Horse?

I-[_] I have my Doubts about that — why would Jesus Christ be Coming on his Great White Horse, when he does not even have a True Church to Come to? Have you not red "Which Church is the Right Church?" (Can all Churches be Correct?) **By The Good Pastor of Uncommon Sense!** Book 119? I Plan on going to Heaven, when I Die by Grace.

J-[_] Justice Demands that we Tax Slaves DEMAND: "The GREAT Worldwide TELEVISED Court HEARING!" (That Great Meeting of the Most-Intelligent and Well-Educated Minds!) By The Worldwide People's Revolution!® Book 041B, whereby we might Learn the WHOLE Truth about all such Important Subjects, including WHO was in Charge of bringing Down the World Trade Center

(WTC) Towers during September 11th, 2001, before we all go to Hell with Satan, the Devil, who has Obviously Deceived most of us. For Example, the Lying Conniving Edomites Falsely Claim that those 283 Hardened Steel Columns SLICED OFF themselves; or, that some Airplanes Sliced them Off at 45-degree Angles, which is Obviously the EXPLOSIVE Work of some Professional Demolition Teams, who used Military-grade Nano-Thermite, which only the Federal Government of "The Divided States of United Lies!" (The so-called "United States of North America" in Disguise!) By The Worldwide People's Revolution!® Book 058, had Access to, which Required no less than 6 Weeks to get 5,000 Tons of it Set Up and Tested for the Grand Day of Marvelous American Deceptions, whose Fake False-Flag Anti-Christ Cover-up Federal Government says that Conspiracy Theories did it! §‡§§

K-[_] King Jesus Knows Exactly WHO did it, and he Revealed it to our Selected KING! ‡

L-[_] Lots of Laughs! King Jesus is nothing more than Jewish Mythology! Have you not even Watched a YouTube Video, called: *ZEITGEIST, the All-American Religious HOAX?*

M-[_] MONEY was at the Bottom of it all. In Fact, there were more than 400 Billion Gold Bricks in the Basement of WTC Tower 7, which came Crashing Down at 5:20 p.m., without any Airplane Striking it, whereby all of those Hardened Steel Columns simply COLLAPSED, in UNISON, like Ballet Dancers hitting the Floor at the same Time, in less than 7 Seconds, at the Smell of Capitalist SMOKE and Mirrors, if you Know what I Mean.§

N-[_] I am such an Ignorant Nitwit, that I never even Heard about WTC Tower 7 coming Down! Are you Sure that **EXPERTS SPEAK OUT** have it Riit, on YouTube Videos? †§‡

O-[_] Are there no Options to Choose from? Could those 283 Hardened Steel Columns not have been Sliced Off by Osama bin Laden and Sons, Incorporated? I Mean, those 19.2 Saudi Arabian Low-jackers with UPS Suits on, had nothing else to Do that Weekend, just before September 11th, 2001, except to Sneak into WTC Towers 1, 2 and 7, and Set Up 5,000 Tons of

Military-grade Nano-Thermite! Indeed, the United Parcel Service (UPS) must have been in on the Grand Conspiracy, without Knowing it, who were Filmed by Video Surveillance Cameras, which were all Destroyed in the Destruction of 9/11/2001.§

P-[_] People like you are Prone to Believe any Conspiracy Lies that anyone can Invent. Why not be Perfectly Honest about it, and bring the Crime to COURT, since NONE of the Accused Criminals were brought to Court, whereby the Real Criminals Escaped, Scot-free. {See the **Appendix** for Meanings of Strange Expressions of Speech in English Nonsense.}

Q-[_] The Great Question is this: **Will we Tax Slaves DEMAND** "The GREAT Worldwide TELEVISED Court HEARING!" (That Great Meeting of the Most-Intelligent and Well-Educated Minds!) By The Worldwide People's Revolution!® Book 041B, as all Righteous People should; or, **will we Allow it to be Covered Up like the President Kennedy Assassination?** What is WRong about getting some True Justice?

R-[_] Republican Reprobates do not Want the Whole Truth to be Revealed: beCause, they are a Part of the Conspiracy to Cover it up, or else they would be Calling for that Great Meeting of the Most-Intelligent and Well-Educated Minds — such as those Architects and Engineers that made up the Video, called: **EXPERTS SPEAK OUT,** on the Internet. †§‡

S-[_] Science has nothing to Do with WHO did it. I say that the Devil did it. Prove me to be WRong, if you can. Otherwise, just Accept the Fact that Osama bin Laden did it. †§‡§§

T-[_] You People are Totally CRAZY! There is only ONE Thing that could have Done it, and that was Military-grade Nano-Thermite, which was Discovered in the Truckloads of DUST that were Gathered up at the Crash Site, which Covered 10 City Blocks! So, Think about it, and Use your Brains for a Change. How did such Dust get there? What Produced such Great CLOUDS of Dust and EXPLOSIVE Debris during September 11th, 2001? †§‡§§

U-[_] I am a Unitarian, and I do not Believe that President George Warmonger Bush, nor Little Dick Chicanery had anything to Do with the Evil Events of September 11ᵗʰ, 2001. §‡

V-[_] So, O Victoria, would you Object to bringing it to COURT, in Order to Prove it, whereby we might Obey the Inspired Words of the Apostle Paul, who wrote: *"Prove all Provable Things, and Cling Tightly to ALL that is GOOD!"* which is still Good Advice? ‡

W-[_] I will Pray that King Solomon Arises from the Dead, whereby that Important Issue might be Settled without World War 3. After all, if it was an All-American False Flag Operation, it is very likely going to Piss Off a LOT of People in this World of Woes, who will be Demanding some True JUSTICE, which will Begin with that Worldwide Meeting.

X-[_] X-number of Ignorant People will Assume that we are talking about some World Court in the Haag; but, we are NOT. We are Talking about a Great Meeting of the Leaders of ALL Major Nations, Worldwide: beCause, "The Divided States of United Lies!" is not the only Nation with Top Secrets that Need to be Exposed in the Bright Light of Good Understanding for everyone to Study. Therefore, we must Address ALL Major Crimes, including WHO Orchestrated the HoloHOAX, and even Persuaded X-number of People to Believe in all such Outlandish Edomite LIES! For Example, it is no Secret that it Requires no less than one Hour, just to Heat Up a Crematory Oven; and then, it Requires no less than 4 to 10 Hours to Thoroughly Cremate an Adult Body, depending on the Age, Size, Weight, and Density of the Bones and Teeths; and then, it Requires another Hour to COOL DOWN the Crematory Oven, just to make it Safe for the Attendants to Open the Door: beCause of the INTENSE HEAT, which would Fry their Eyeballs and Skins, if it were not Cooled Down: beCause those Ovens are more than 4000° Fahrenheit, or 10000° Centigrade! Therefore, it is very Important to get all of the Facts Correct, before we can make any Rational Judgments about anything. Therefore, if you Agree, Check the Boxes [_]. But, if you do not Agree, get yourself Prepared for **The GWTCH:** beCause, we must Prevent **"The Great ATOMIC NIGHTMARE!"** **(The Saddest Story in World History!) By The Great White**

Bald Eagle! Book 099, which will be the Results of Rejecting Provable Truths, which is Explained in: "What is The GREATEST SIN?" (And it is NOT Blasphemy Against the Holy Spirit!) By The Worldwide People's Revolution!® Book 091. Indeed, no such Evil Things Happen without Justified CAUSES. Therefore, do not Deceive yourself any longer: beCause these and those Evil Things must be EXPOSED: beCause Liberation can only come by "The Swanky Sword of Divine Truths!" (The Most-Powerful Weapon in the Whole Universe!) By The Worldwide People's Revolution!® Book 067. Therefore, Believe it, and Accept it, whereby you can be made Happy by it, which Requires a FULL CONFESSION of ALL Provable Truths. §‡

Y-[_] I Remember when a certain Young Man Lied about his Fornication with a certain Young Womb-man, who was found Pregnant within a few Months, whereby his Lies were Exposed, which Cause him to be most Ashamed of himself, later on, when the Baby Grew Up and Discovered that his Father was just a LIAR. However, if he had made his Confession, right away, and got Married to that Woman, no one would have Known that he did anything WRong, which would have Saved the entire Family from a Lot of Shame.

Z-[_] The Great ZEAL of "The Worldwide People's Revolution!" (A Comprehensive Plan for Obtaining Worldwide Law, Order, Obedience, Peace and True Prosperity!) By The Worldwide People's Revolution!® B-108, will Liberate all of us, if we have it. ‡

00-10 [_] O Doctor Samuel Walker Edison, was it just Coincidental that all of those Statements just Happened to Work Out with the ABC's; or, was that something that you Manipulated, yourself? Why is it that I do not Trust you, nor your Selected King, who is Professional at that? §‡

The Enticing MENU on the Table of Contents
for a Satisfying Feast of Provable Truths!

{HEADNOTE: This Inspired Book contains a few Photographs with Explanations, plus about 30,000 Words that should be Proven at: **The GWTCH!** Moreover, if you do not know what that Means, it Means that you Skipped Over the Copyright, Dedication and Introduction, Oh Cheater.}

{Missing Chapters will be Supplied when they are Needed.}

FOOTNOTE: The Symbols (†§‡§§) are Explained in: "Which Church is the Right Church?" (Can all Churches be Correct?) By The Good Pastor of Uncommon Sense! Book 119. It wil not Kil uu to Reed it. See the KEE TQ PROONUNSEEAASHUN in: "LIGHTNING STRIKES Versus Lightning Bugs!" (HOW you can Become Moderately RICH, without Telling any Lies nor Selling any Trash!) By The Worldwide People's Revolution!® Book 074.

ATTENTION: If some of the Words or Photos are too small to read with Comfort, please see the 8.5 by 11-inch Colored Edition, which has print this Size, in 12 Points, instead of 10. That Book is also less Expensive than the 6 by 9-inch Colored Edition: beCause of having fewer Sheets of Paper. It also has a few Corrections that are not in this Edition: beCause of being more Scrupulously Proof-red by our Team. Moreover, that larger Edition also has every Paragraph Justified, whereby each Verse Ends at the End of the Line, which is one of only 2 or 3 of my Books that do that in all Cases, which will make it a Good Collector's Item: beCause it is Unique in that Way, being so Inspired as to Do that. †§‡

— Chapter 02 —

Why is Chapter 01 Missing?

02-01 [_] The Missing Chapter 01 is only Symbolical of the Missing Books in your own Mind, which you have yet to Study. For Example, someone called "Moses" wrote *Genesis, Exodus, Numbers, Leviticus and Deuteronomy,* while leaving Out *Good Government,* "The Seven Basic Spiritual Building Blocks of LIFE!" (Faith Hope Trust Love Patience Persistence and Obedience!) By The Worldwide People's Revolution!® Book 036, "God Speaks and the Whole World Listens!" (Fire on the Mountain from the Burning Bush by the Spirit of Truths!) By The Worldwide People's Revolution!® Book 026B, "In thu Beeginingz uv Thingz!" (Thu Kreeaashun Stooree frum thu Beegining!) By The Worldwide People's Revolution!® Book 025B, "IMPORTANT THINGS that Should Have Been Written in the Holy Bible!" (A Special Challenge to all Professing Christians, Jews, Hindus, Muslims and Atheists!) **By** The Irreverent Penname Scumbag! Book 110, and a Long List of other Fascinating Literature that should be put into that *Holy Bible,* which is not even one-tenth as Long as it should be for 12-year-old Children to Understand what is Required for Worldwide Law, Order, Obedience, Peace and True Prosperity, which should begin with the Construction of those "GLORIOUS Swanky Hotels Castles and Fortresses!" (Beautiful Planned City States for WISE Intelligent Well-Educated People with Common Sense and Good Understanding!) By The Worldwide People's Revolution!® Book 019B: beCause, they will Solve BILLIONS of Problems — considering the Fact that each Person has his or her own Problems, which cannot be Solved without such Fortresses. For Example, how many Houses Heat and Cool themselves by Solar Power, even as they all should? (Please take your Time to Study the Following Drawings.)

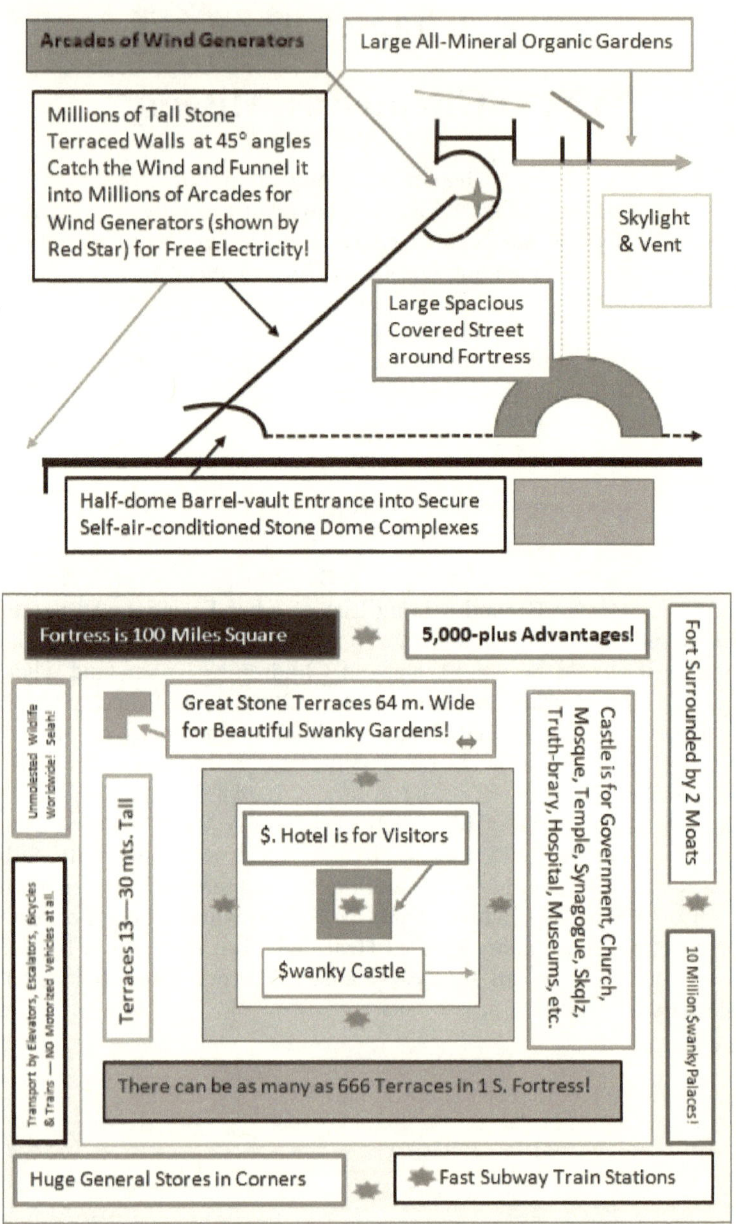

02-02 [_] O Selected King of **The Worldwide People's Revolution,** just how Painful would it have been for "Moses," Joshua, or someone else, to have put those Rough Drawings into that so-called *"Holy Bible,"* whereby we Tax Slaves might have Studied those Drawings, and thus, Discovered how to Save for ourselves TRILLIONS of Wasted Dollars? For Example, when a Rat or a Mouse gets into your House, from leaving the Door Standing Wide Open, all that you have to Do is to Find that Mouse or Rat, Cast him OUT, and Close the Door. Likewise, if a Bad Person Happens to get Born Inside of a Swanky Fortress, and you cannot Correct him with Good Sermons, you only have to Discover him, and BANISH him from the Fortress, whereby he is no longer a Problem, which Means that you do not have to Tax the People within that City of Peace, for Hiring a Police DEPARTment: beCause no such Policemen are Needed, nor Wanted, which is GOOD. ‡

02-03 [_] Well, my Friend, that is Exactly what I have been Telling People for more than 40 Years; but, it seems that they have Ears that cannot Hear very Well. Perhaps they are Afraid that they will also be Discovered to be Outlaws, who might also get Banished for Stealing a Cookie or Candy Bar, which could Prove to be very Em-bare-assing, you might say — except that such Minor Offenses only Require a Strapping on the Buttocks by a Father who has some Good Understanding.

02-04 [_] O Unelected King of "The Worldwide People's Revolution!" (A Comprehensive Plan for Obtaining Worldwide Law, Order, Obedience, Peace and True Prosperity!) By The Worldwide People's Revolution!® Book 108, are you Sure that such Violent Reactions by a Revengeful Father will not Cause all of his Children to HATE him for so Cruelly Punishing them?

02-05 [_] Well, my Potential Friend, or Potential Enemy, all Punishments should be Administered with the Consent of whomever is being Punished, if the Child is more than 11 Years Old: beCause, any 12-year-old Child should Know Better than to Steal any Cookies, Candies, Cakes, Cokes, or other Sweet Things that might Rot Out his Precious Teeth: beCause he will Need his Teeth for the Remainder of his Life. Therefore, if he Judges that Stealing a Candy Bar was not such a Bad Thing, he should be Fairly WARNED about the Dangers of Refined Sugar, and Asked: "What should your Punishment be for Stealing that Candy Bar?" — at which Time he might say, 'I Know that the Sugar is no Good for my Teeth; but, I Intended to Brush my Teeth after Eating it, even though I did not have my Toothbrush with me, in "The Public School of IGNERUNT FOLZ!" (HOW we have been GRAATLEE DISEEVD by Capitalism!) By The Worldwide People's

Revolution!® Book 024B.' And then his Father might say, "So, why are you now Lying to me?"

02-06 [_] O Selected King of **The Worldwide People's Revolution**, you must be a Near Relative of King Solomon, himself. Would you Actually Expect that Rebellious Son to say, "I should get no less than 3 Lashes with a Razor Strap, or a Wide Leather Belt, just for Disobeying you"? †§‡§§

02-07 [_] Well, my Friend, he should Know the Degree of his own Stubbornness, and also Understand what is Required to Straighten himself Out. Therefore, 3 or 5 Lashes might Fix him.‡

02-08 [_] O Elected King of **"The New RIGHTEOUS One-World Government!" (HOW to Establish a Righteous One-World Government without Going to WAR!) By The Worldwide People's Revolution!® Book 056**, I Hope to God that you are in Charge of Things around here for at least a thousand Years to Come: beCause, if I Rob a Bank for a Million Dollars, I will Judge that my Punishment should be a Gold Medal of Honor: beCause of getting just a little Justice for the Trillions of Dollars that those Greedy Edomite Bankers have Stolen from the Masses of People, who do not even Realize that a RIGHTEOUS Government has NO NEED for ANY BANKERS!

02-09 [_] Well, my Friend, without Bankers, how would a Poor Person ever be Able to Buy a Hut?

02-10 [_] Well, O King Solomon, that Question was already Answered in one of those Deleted Books that used to be in the *Unholy Mutilated Bible* — such as *The Book of the Wars of the LORD, The Book of Nathan the Prophet, The Book of Shemaiah, The Book of Jehu, The Book of Gad, The Book of Asher, The Books of Enoch, The Book of the Acts of King Solomon, First and Last.* Yes, the *Holy Bible* even Mentions those Books by Name, as well as *The Book of Jasher, The Prophecies of Ahijah the Shilonite, The Book of Iddo,* and *The Book of Moses,* which Jesus Referred to; and *The First Epistle to the Laodiceans,* which is Suggesting that the Apostle Paul most likely Wrote several Important Letters, which were Deleted by whomever Constructed the *Unholy Mutilated Bible,* which Suggests that there were THOUSANDS of Missing Books, and not just a few Missing Chapters. For Example, not one of the *Old Testament Scriptures,* which are Mentioned in *Matthew 2,* concerning the Coming of Jesus, can be Found in the *Old Testament!* §‡ (See *Numbers 21:14; Joshua 10:13; Second Samuel 1:18; Second Chronicles*

9:9, 29; 12:15; 13:22; Ester 8:13; and Related Scriptures. What about all of the Thots that are never Finished? ‡)

— Chapter 03 —

WHY
Beautiful Planned City States
will have to be Built!

03-01 [_] The Short Answer is very Simple — there is no other Way to Solve those 5,000 Massive Problems — such as Traffic Accidents, which are followed by a Long List of Bad Chain-Reactions.

03-02 [_] O Selected King of "The Worldwide People's Revolution!" (A Comprehensive Plan for Obtaining Worldwide Law, Order, Obedience, Peace and True Prosperity!) By The Worldwide People's Revolution!® Book 108, I Hate to have to Confess it; but, I have no Idea what a Chain-Reaction is. Therefore, would you Object to Explaining it to us Transportation Slaves? After all, we are far too Slow to Learn our Lessons, as God might have Intended it. †§‡§§

03-03 [_] Well, my Friend, at First Appearance, it might Look like a little Harmless Accident; but, let me take us through the entire Evil Chain-Reaction — except the Long List of Police Actions, Tickets, Trials, etc., etc., whereby you might have some Idea what all is brought about by Making and Selling Vehicles of Various Kinds, including Wagons that are Drawn by Run-away Horses. ‡

A-[_] Mr. Proud Smart Investor Buys a Car for himself and his Ignorant Family, who are so Happy to be the Proud Owners of some Capitalist Junk, on its Way to the Junkyard. ‡

B-[_] A Half-Drunk Driver "goes through a red light," and Causes a School Bus to Crash into his Truck: beCause of having a Green Light, which made it Legal; but, not at all Safe.

C-[_] 40 Children are Injured, and the Bus Driver and 4 Children in Front Seats are Killed.

D-[_] 6 Ambulances are Called during the Rush Hour. 2 of them run through Red Lights, causing 8 Innocent Victims to get Killed in 4 Cars. Ambulance Squads are Demobilized.

E-[_] Wounded Children on the Bus Telephoned their Parents, some of whom Rushed to the Crash Site, who also Drove through Red Lights with Horns Honking; but, 3 of them got into Accidents, and 2 of them got Killed, whose Children Lived to Grieve about it.

F-[_] The Fatalities were Credited to Cheap Cars; but, that did not Pay the Insurance Bills.

G-[_] Many People Prayed to God for Help; but, he seemed to be Sleeping at the Time. Some of the Children on the Bus had Head Injuries, 2 of them are still in Comas for months.

H-[_] The Drunk Driver in the Dump Truck was Injured; but, not Killed. He was Sued for Damages; but, being so Poor and not a Property Owner, and without Insurance, he Escaped.

I-[_] Insurance did Cover the Children in the School Bus, and Paid for their Funerals; but, it never Comforted their Grieving Parents, the Victimized Families, Friends, nor Relatives.

J-[_] Justice was the Victim in all of it: beCause no one got any True Justice, which Requires the Whole Truth, and nothing but the Whole Truth: beCause, it is Possible that 99.9% of the People would Willingly Choose to Liv within Swanky Fortresses, if they were given the Opportunity to VOTE for it, after Learning all of the Great Advantages: beCause of having many Debates about it, who, as of this Date, have never Heard about Swanky Fortresses: beCause the Subject has never been brought up in Congress, nor in Newspapers.

K-[_] Not even Kings nor Queens are Exempt from those Horrible Car Accidents. Princess Diana should know all about that, among several other "Rich" Victims of Kinetic Energy.

L-[_] Lots of Laughs! People are not going to Stop Driving Cars, just beCause they are Dangerous: beCause, they have to get to Work on Time, in spite of Traffic Jams and Speed Limits: beCause that is the American Way of Progress, which is Retrogression at its Best.

M-[_] The Medics had to Deal with the Blood and Guts of all of those Accidents, which made them Sick, which probably Helped to make them into Alcoholics, just for Relief from it: beCause of all of the Needless STRESS, which is also Common among Medics with the Bug-19, which is even more Stressful than Treating the Victims of Vehicular Accidents. ‡

N-[_] If everyone Lived within those **"GLORIOUS Swanky Hotels Castles and Fortresses!"** the Bug would be nothing but a Joke: beCause, everyone could Lock their Doors and Stay at Home, and Work in their Gardens and Home-craft Workshops, until the Viirus is DEAD. Indeed, any Nitwit would Know that much about it. Chances are that most of those Swanky Fortresses would never get Infected with any Viirusez of any Kinds. †§‡

O-[_] Operations on Wounded Bodies is NOT Cheap. One of those Victims Costed the Government more than 2 Million Dollars, and she is still not Healed! It is INSANITY! †§‡

P-[_] Most People LOVE their Cars and Pickup Trucks, and would never Consider Sacrificing them to Junkyards. § However, if a War broke out, they would Cheerfully Sacrifice them for Bullets and Bombs, and especially if the Automotive Industry was Threatened: beCause it is the Primary Source of American Prosperity, Worldwide. Selah.‡

Q-[_] The Great Question is: **When will we RUN OUT of Gasoline and Motor Oil?** — 100 Years from now, 200 Years from now, or 400 Years from now? When we do, that will be the END of the Car Industry: beCause there will be no more Cheap Fuel to BURN! †§‡

R-[_] Fire Engines had to be Called to come to the Accidents: beCause several Vehicles got on Fire. Therefore, that Caused a lot of Negative Chain-Reactions and Hidden Costs. ‡

S-[_] Saint Peter would not Object to Living within those **"GLORIOUS Swanky Hotels Castles and Fortresses!"** with Saint Paul: beCause they both Liked to WALK. In Fact, Saint Paul Walked more than 10,000 Miles as a Missionary around the Mediterranean Sea.

T-[_] The Total Costs of that one Accident will most likely never be Known: beCause, for Example, the Stress has its own Evil Chain-Reactions, which will Linger on for Decades!

U-[_] I Understand that a certain Amount of Stress is Good for People, which keeps them Awake, when they should be Sleeping, which makes Horror Stories and Spooky Movies so GOOD, which add many Years to our Lives, and keeps us on our Toes, as they say. †§§

V-[_] O Victory in Jesus, who came to Save us from the Sins of Self-Deceptions and Lies.

W-[_] I would rather go to WAR, than to give up my Holy Car, which helps to Destroy the Atmosphere, and Raise the Temperature of the Whole World. Praise Buzzeldick the Great!

X-[_] X-number of People are just plain STUPID. Indeed, if Swanky Fortresses will Raise our Standard of Living by 10,000 Times, then that is the Way to Prosper, and right away!‡

Y-[_] I am Yearning for **"The GREAT Worldwide TELEVISED Court HEARING!"** (That Great Meeting of the Most-Intelligent and Well-Educated Minds!) By The Worldwide People's Revolution!® Book 041B, just to Hear all of the Amazing Arguments over this Inflammable Issue, which is Bound to Win in Favor of **"The Environmentalists' Perfect Paradise!"** (HOW almost Everyone can be Living in a Beautiful Manmade Paradise!) By The Worldwide People's Revolution!® Book 035C.

Z-[_] The Zeal of "The Worldwide People's Revolution!" (A Comprehensive Plan for Obtaining Worldwide Law, Order, Obedience, Peace and True Prosperity!) By The Worldwide People's Revolution!® Book 108, will make all of that Possible and GOOD.

03-04 [_] O Selected King of the Mountains, Courthouse Record Books have Case after Case of Bad Things to say about Capitalism, which is the Love of Money in Action. For Example, I have a Cousin, who owns a Used-Car Sales Lot, who Sells Cars that are not Fit to be on the Highway, and he Knows it; but, he Sells them, anyway: beCause he is so Poor, and does not know what else to Do for a Living: beCause his Daddy was in that same Evil Business, and Died in a Car Wreck.

03-05 [_] Well, he most likely Died from Lighting Up a Stinking Cigarette: beCause they are the Cause for a LOT of Accidents: beCause of taking their Eyes Off of the Highway for a Second / 2.

03-06 [_] O Selected King, I would say that all such People Deserve such Just Rewards — except that there are so many Innocent People who get Hurt, or Killed, by the Selfishness of other People.

03-07 [_] Therefore, that is the Primary Reason for Wise People to MOVE OUT of all such Cities of Confusion, and MOVE INTO those "Beautiful Swanky PALACES!" (A New Concept in Living Habits — Swanky Palaces for Poor People!) By The Worldwide People's Revolution!® Book 066, where it is Impossible to get Killed by any Dangerous Vehicles: beCause they have none. Therefore, if anyone Refuses to Check the above Box with a LARGE GREEN-X Mark, such a Person is Suspect of being INSANE! However, if you do not Think so, just Continue to Liv in one of those Stinking, Noisy, Polluted Cities of Massive Confusion, and Enjoy all of the Evil News Broadcasts as much as you can: beCause, it will not be long before almost all Cities of Confusion are Abandoned! {See: "The END of CONFUSION!" (The Great CELEBRATION of the Magnificent Wedding of the Most-Humble, Honest Nations, and the Grand Year of JUBILEE!) By The Worldwide People's Revolution!® Book 050. [_] Amen.}

03-08 [_] O Selected King, they should Especially Study: "HOW Righteousness can Overcome Wickedness!" (The Triumph of the Soul who Knows God!) By The Enlightened Professor of Common Sense! B-093: beCause that is most Practical, and a Good Civilized Way of Doing it. ‡

03-09 |_| Well, my Friend, I Dare say that 100 Years from now, there will be no large Cities of Confusion in all of the World; but, first of all, we must get RID of those Lying Conniving Edomites: beCause they are the Roadblock to True Progress on the Highway of Life and Death. ‡

03-10 [_] And, O Selected King, just Exactly HOW do you Plan on getting Rid of those Edomites?

{Here is an Example of what they "Created" for us, Legally, for "Profit," they say: https://youtu.be/-dk3NOEgX7o Plastic Wars by FRONTLINE. There is plenty of Space below here for more Links, if you have some to Share with us. See our E-mail Address on Back Cover.}

Here is a Link for everyone to Study: https://youtu.be/HYNB4sAxemk called: History of the Black Death. Just do not Forget to Return to this Book when you get Finished with that History Lesson.

— Chapter 04 —

HOW to get Rid of those Lying Conniving Edomites!

04-01 [_] First of all, the Tax Slaves and all other Slaves, must DEMAND: "The GREAT Worldwide TELEVISED Court HEARING!" (That Great Meeting of the Most-Intelligent and Well-Educated Minds!) By The Worldwide People's Revolution!® Book 041B, whereby I can Ask all of the Leaders of all Major Nations a few Important Questions:

A-[_] Do any of you Leaders DENY that we are Blest with Sufficient Mountains of Rocks, whereby everyone in the Whole World could be Living within their own Private and "Beautiful Swanky Stone Dome Home COMPLEXES!" (HOW to Build SECURE Tax-proof, Insurance-proof, Self-air-conditioned, Paint-proof, Rot-proof, Termite-proof, Mouse-proof, Fireproof, Tornado-proof, Hurricane-proof, Thief-proof, and BOMB-PROOF Houses!) By The Worldwide People's Revolution!® Book 102? If you Deny it, please STAND UP! — at which Time none of them will Stand Up: beCause they all Know for a Fact that we have Plenty of Building Materials for making no less than 2 Million of those "GLORIOUS Swanky Hotels Castles and Fortresses!" (Beautiful Planned City States for WISE Intelligent Well-Educated People with Common Sense and Good Understanding!) By The Worldwide People's Revolution!® Book 019B. †§‡

B-[_] Do any of you Leaders DENY that we have Sufficient Technologies for Building all such Beautiful Planned City States? If you Deny it, please STAND UP! — at which Time none of them will Stand Up: beCause they all Know for a Fact that we can Do it, if we Want to; and, the Vast Majority of the People Want to, just to get to Eat at those: "Royal Swanky Buffets!" (The Best Feasts in the Whole World!) By The Worldwide People's Revolution!® Book 103, which will have more than a thousand Delicious Dishes of Wholesome Natural Foods to Choose from, including 100% Pure Iced-creamed-Mangos!

C-|_| Do any of you Leaders DENY that we have any less than 4 Billion Young People, who would be Happy to Help Build those Swanky Fortresses, if they were Paid According to "A List of FAIR Swanky Wages!" (The Equitable Wage System!) By The Worldwide People's Revolution!® Book 065? If you DENY it, please STAND UP! — at which Time none of them will Dare to Stand Up: beCause those "Seven Great Armies of Working Soldiers!" (HOW to Provide a Way for Everyone to WORK: so as to Eliminate Poverty, Crimes, Drug Abuses, Prisons and Unnecessary Taxes!) By The Worldwide People's Revolution!® Book 015B, and "The Swanky Associations of Working Soldiers!" (A Fascinating Collection of Various Kinds of Voluntary Working Soldiers!) By The Worldwide People's Revolution!® Book 018B, will be Filling the Streets of Rome with their Picks, Shovels, Spud Bars, Hammers, Axes, Meat Cleavers, Butcher Knives, Meat Grinders, Chainsaws, Drills, Vices, Screwdrivers, Saws, Wheelbarrows, Scythes, Machetes, Pitch Forks, Rakes, Trowels, Levels, Plumb Bobs, Squares, Drawing Boards, Instruction Books, and whatever they Need for making Dog Foods and Hog Slop from the Carcasses of those so-called "Leaders," who will soon come to their Right Senses, and: "VOTE for The GOAT!" (The New Political Party that has Guaranteed Solutions for our Massive Problems!) By The Worldwide People's Revolution!® Book 109: beCause, that is the only Practical Thing to Do! After all, they are Sick of "Poverty Hunger Riots Strikes Police Brutalities Election Deceptions and Civil Wars!" (The High Price that we Earthlings have Paid for Leaving the Good Land!) By The Worldwide People's Revolution!® Book 014B. Yes, they have Red: "Are you a Jobless Graduate of the SKQL uv FQLZ?" (HOW to Get a GOUD EJUKAASHUN without Robbing the Bank!) By The Worldwide People's Revolution!® Book 020B, which is a Companion Book of: "Does a Good Soldier have to be a MURDERER?" (Seven Great Swanky Armies of Voluntary Working Soldiers!) By The Worldwide People's Revolution!® Book 027B. Therefore, they will be Ready to Chop, Slice, Grind, Boil, Bake, Barbecue, Fry, Drill Holes in their Heads, and Dung on their Heads, if they do not Answer Honestly, without any Political Nonsense! §‡

D-|_| Do any of you Rich Bankers DENY that it is the Duty of "The New **RIGHTEOUS** One-World Government!" (**HOW to Establish a Righteous One-World Government without Going to WAR!**) **By The Worldwide People's Revolution!®** Book 056, to Mint and Print the Necessary New Money, with New Faces and New Numbers, for the Purpose of HIRING those "**Seven Great Armies of Working Soldiers!**" to Help one another to Build those "**GLORIOUS Swanky Hotels Castles and Fortresses!**" for everyone in the Whole World, who Wants to Liv in PEACE with True Security? If you Deny it, please STAND UP! — at which Time, none of them will Dare to Stand Up: beCause their Evil Heads will be put on the Chopping Blocks for the Meat Cleavers to Sever: beCause, their Services will no longer be Needed by anyone! And all of the Righteous People will SHOUT for JOY: beCause their Days of Surviving as Interest and Usury Slaves will be OVER! †§‡

04-02 |_| O Elected King of "The New **RIGHTEOUS** One-World Government!" (**HOW to Establish a Righteous One-World Government without Going to WAR!**) **By The Worldwide People's Revolution!®** Book 056, I must Confess that if you ever get into that Position of Authority by a Democratic Election, those Lying Conniving Edomites will be Hunting in the Mountains for Caves to Crawl into, even if they are Occupied by Grizzly Bears: beCause, there will be no Safe Place for them to Hide themselves: beCause of their Robberies of Interest Slaves!

04-03 [_] Well, my Friend, all that they will have to Do to Escape from the WRATH of those Abused Work Slaves with Pistols and Rifles in their Hands, is to Adopt New Names, and Join "**The Swanky Associations of Working Soldiers!**" (**A Fascinating Collection of Various Kinds of Voluntary Working Soldiers!**) **By The Worldwide People's Revolution!®** Book 018B, and we will Forgive them for all of their Monetary Crimes: beCause, they did not Realize what they were Doing to the Masses of Education Slaves, Work Slaves, Tax Slaves, Credit Card Debt Slaves, Insurance Slaves, Home-owner Slaves, Interest Slaves, Mortgage Slaves, Transportation Bills Slaves, Repair Bills Slaves, Telephone Bills Slaves, Childcare Slaves, and all of those other Kinds of SLAVES that were only Mentioned in Verse 00-09-F. Indeed, they should make their Full Confessions in Books, and Publish them on Amazon Books, just to let us Know that they are Sincerely Repenting, and Want to Change their Ways of Living, and Adopt the Swanky Fortress System, which has NO Slaves of any Kinds! For Example, if someone Wants to Learn HOW to put Together Fine Hand-carved Leather-bound Books, they only Need to Study: "LIGHTNING STRIKES Versus Lightning Bugs!" (HOW you can Become Moderately RICH, without Telling any Lies nor Selling any Trash!) By The Worldwide People's Revolution!® Book 074.

04-04 [_] O Selected King, would they not also Need some Good Teachers, who can Assist them to Learn that Leather-carving Business, without Wasting any Time in "The Public School of IGNERUNT FQLZ!" (HOW we have been GRAATLEE DISEEVD by Capitalism!) By The Worldwide People's Revolution!® Book 024B? Why not begin now to Train some Young Men?

04-05 [_] Yes, of course, my Friend, they would Need the Best of Good Teachers for whatever Crafts that they might Want to Learn, who are called Master Craftsmen, who Deserve the Best of Good Swanky Wages! Therefore, they will be the Envy of the World, once they Learn their Craft!

04-06 [_] For Example, there is a 400-year-old German Desk, made with Hand-operated Tools, without any Paints. The Different Colors are made from Different Kinds of Woods. Just Compare that Desk with those of Poor Office Workers, nowadays, who have not even Seen such Desks for Sale: beCause, Capitalism could never Afford to make one. However, when those Working Soldiers have Retired, after only 6 Years of Common Skilled Labor, and are Living in their "Beautiful Swanky PALACES!" (A New Concept in Living Habits — Swanky Palaces for Poor People!) By The Worldwide People's Revolution!® Book 066, they will have lots of Time to Play in their Home-craft Workshops with Well-made Swanky Tools, which they can Discover for FREE at any Swanky Tool Houses: beCause, all Tools, including Computers, Televisions, Radios, and Special Craft Tools will be FREE for anyone who is Trained to Use them: beCause that will Provide a Way for TRUE PROSPERITY! Moreover, there will also be **"The Swanky Association of Professional All-Mineral Organic Gardeners,"** who will be Growing Billions of Tons of Fruits, Nuts, Vegetables, and Flowers, according to: "The LUSCIOUS All-Mineral Organic Method of Gardening!" (HOW to Grow DELICIOUS Satisfying Foods for Potential Kingz and Kweenz in Beautiful Swanky PALACES!) By The Worldwide People's Revolution!® Book 021B, which is a Companion Book of: "Orgimmick Gardening at its Best!" (HOW to Grow Delicious Satisfying Foods without a 10-Million-Dollar Investment!) By The Worldwide People's Revolution!® Book 079. In other Words, you will be Welcome to Attend to your own One-Acre (210-feet by 210-feet) All-Mineral Organic Garden with 3 to 4 feet of Rich Topsoil; or, you can Invite **"The Swanky Association of Professional All-Mineral Organic Gardeners"** to Attend to it, for FREE; but, no matter who you are, if you are Physically and Mentally Able, you will have to Do at least 4 Hours of Common Skilled Labor per Workday, or the Equivalent thereof — such as 8 Hours Today, and Tomorrow Off; or, Work this Week for 8 Hours per Day, and take Off next Week; or, Work this Month, and take Off next Month, etc., etc.

04-07 [_] O Elected King of **"The New RIGHTEOUS One-World Government!"** will there be a Voluntary Army of Working Soldiers for each Necessary Occupation? For Example, will there be one Special Army that does nothing but Grow Good Foods to Eat, which Feeds the other Voluntary Armies of Working Soldiers? May I Join **"The Swanky Association of Professional Cooks and Chefs"** — since I just LOVE those DELICIOUS Home-made Dill Pickles and Honey-roasted Peanuts, and especially those Green-chili PISTACHIOS? Will I get to Eat all that I Want?

04-08 [_] Well, my Friend, it will take a while for the Fruit and Nut Trees to Grow Up, as well as the Children who will be Eating from them; but, once we get everything going Well, you will get to Eat all that you Want and Lust after at those "Royal Swanky Buffets!" (The Best Feasts in the Whole World!) By The Worldwide People's Revolution!® Book 103. Moreover, if you get too Fat, you may Attend one of those "Beautiful Swanky FASTING SANITARIUMS!" (HOW to Learn Good Self-Discipline!) **By** The Worldwide People's Revolution!® Book 115. †§‡§§

04-09 [_] O Elected King of **"The New RIGHTEOUS One-World Government!"** will we have to BUY our own "Beautiful Swanky Stone Dome Home COMPLEXES!" (HOW to Build SECURE Tax-proof, Insurance-proof, Self-air-conditioned, Paint-proof, Rot-proof, Termite-proof, Mouse-proof, Fireproof, Tornado-proof, Hurricane-proof, Thief-proof, and BOMB-PROOF Houses!) By The Worldwide People's Revolution!® Book 102, just to Liv in?

04-10 [_] Well, my Friend, I would not Think of Delivering you from one Form of Slavery, into another Form of Slavery: beCause that would Prove to be a very MEAN Trick of the Devil, I would say. Therefore, be Patient, and I will Explain to you just HOW we will Do it, if you do not Object. Here is a Picture of my Onyx Floor, which got Stolen from me by Tricky Capitalist HOGS. You can Learn most of the Details in: "LIGHTNING STRIKES Versus Lightning Bugs!" (HOW you can Become Moderately RICH, without Telling any Lies nor Selling any Trash!) By The Worldwide People's Revolution!® Book 074, which also contains a LOT of Wonderful Things, including: **"The New MAGNIFIED Version of the 20 Commandments!"** for Free, considering the Fact that I was not Compelled by any TYRANT to put them into that Book! †§‡§§

Belgiculture!

— Chapter 05 —

How Poor People can Afford Beautiful Swanky Palaces!

05-01 [_] First of all, we Liberated Tax Slaves must CLAIM our own Mountains of Rocks, Rivers of Water, Minerals, Metals, Gases, Oils, Trees, Topsoils, and whatever God Provided for us, for Free, in Order to SHARE those Good Things with one another: beCause, we are not going to Allow any Greedy Selfish Lying Conniving Edomites to SELL any such Things to us: beCause that Evil Economic System is DEAD and Buried! Yes, we will put it into its Graveyard, at: "The GREAT Worldwide TELEVISED Court HEARING!" (That Great Meeting of the Most-Intelligent and Well-Educated Minds!) By The Worldwide People's Revolution!® Book 041B, which will be "The END of CONFUSION!" (The Great CELEBRATION of the Magnificent Wedding of the Most-Humble, Honest Nations, and the Grand Year of JUBILEE!) By The Worldwide People's Revolution!® Book 050, and the Beginning of Great Peace and True Prosperity, like the Lying Trumpeter has never Heard of: beCause of not Reading, "C-SPAN-DEX!" (Your Filtered View of Bad Government!) By The Worldwide People's Revolution!® Book 097, which gives his entire Orlando Campaign Speech, along with my Corrections and Inspired Words of Provable Truths, many of which you can Discover in Amazon Books, for FREE, if you just Look for them!

05-02 [_] Secondly, once we Establish "The New RIGHTEOUS One-World Government!" we will have an Unlimited Supply of New Money to Work with, which must be EARNED by Honest Labor, without any Loans, without any Interest, without any Usury, and without any Income Taxes.

05-03 [_] O Elected King, that Sounds like BELGICULTURE, to me, which puts everyone on the same Level, or Playing Field, even if they are Related with Poor Nigger Jim, who never Graduated from "The Public School of IGNERUNT FQLZ!" (HOW we have been GRAATLEE DISEEVD by Capitalism!) By The Worldwide People's Revolution!® Book 024B. After all, Black and Brown Peoples are generally the Hardest-working People in this World of Woes, even if they have no Idea what they are Doing: beCause they LOVE to WORK, which makes them Feel Good about themselves. Therefore, they only

Need some GOOD Reliable Masters, to Instruct them concerning what and how to Do it, who may be anyone of any Color, Race, Sex, or whatever. †§‡

05-04 |_| Well, my Friend, before anyone can Join "The Swanky Associations of Working Soldiers!" they must Fill Out and File: "The Complete SURVEYS of our VALUES!" (SURVEYS of Religious Spiritual Political Governmental Sexual Social Moral Economical Business Labor Habitual and Miscellaneous VALUES!) By The Worldwide People's Revolution!® Book 059, whereby we can Discover where they Belong in the Swanky Fortress Economic System, if only to Hoe Weeds in an Organic Garden for 60 Dollars per Hour! But, only IF they Do it Correctly for 4 Hours, which can be Tiresome. However, they will be Free to Do it for 2 Hours during the Cool Time of the Morning, and 2 more Hours during the Cool Time of the Evening, if they Want to Do it that Way, since they will be Good Trustworthy People, if they Check the Appropriate Boxes in the Surveys of their Values. After all, we are not Asking them to be SAINTS; but, only to be HONEST and Trustworthy: beCause, if they are not, they might be BANISHED to some Lower Order of Swanky Fortresses, where they can be Watched by Surveillance Cameras, just to make Sure that they are not Cheating the System in some Way, which is not at all Necessary: beCause 4 Hours of Labor, in Exchange for Living within those "Beautiful Swanky PALACES!" (A New Concept in Living Habits — Swanky Palaces for Poor People!) By The Worldwide People's Revolution!® Book 066, seems to be Perfectly Fair to me. [_] Amen

05-05 [_] For Example, I Dug Up all of those Irish Potatoes during just 4 Hours, and Washed them during the next 4 Hours, while Sitting under my Fig Tree, in the Shade, which were enough Potatoes for Feeding me, and my Loving Brother Vern, all of the Potatoes that we wanted for the next Year. Therefore, why should I make a Slave of myself to some Capitalist, just to Feed myself for a Year?

05-06 [_] O Elected King of "The New RIGHTEOUS One-World Government!" if we just put that False Ownership Doctrine of the Devil into the Trash Can, and Claimed our own Mountains of Rocks, Topsoil in the Louisiana Delta, and Forgot about Wages of any Kind, we could make Beautiful Planned City States for ourselves, and be Done with all Forms of Slavery: beCause, we would have no Use for those Lying Conniving Edomites and their Money Games, who are Determined to Fill Up the Oceans with their Capitalist TRASH, instead of Filling Up their Pantries with Canned Jars of Good Foods, and Filling Up their Root Cellars with all Kinds of Tasty Fruits and Vegetables. However, I am Worried that certain Edomites will be Seeking Revenge for putting them OUT of Business. For Example, they could Volunteer to be Organic Gardeners, who go around with Sharp Pocket Knives, Cutting Gashes into Fruit and Nut Trees, Grape Vines and Berry Bushes, in order to make Ways for Bacterias and Bad Bugs to get into those Trees and Vines, and thus, Ruin them! Therefore, it is very Important to have Garden Inspectors to Constantly Check Up on them: beCause some of them are True Niggers, who Deserve Time behind Steel Bars; but, I Prefer the Leather-Strap Correction-Plan: beCause, it is much more Humane and Civilized. †§‡

05-07 [_] Well, my Friend, just as soon as we Discover such a Nigger, no matter what his or her Color might be, we will make a Public Display of that Person, and Whip his Naked Ass, until he cannot Sit Down on it, as a WARNING to any other Would-be Niggers, like him. After all, if anyone has a Legitimate Complaint, they should Address it to: "FREEDUM uv SPEECH!" (U Speshoul Maguzeen uv Onist Upinyunz!) By The Worldwide People's Revolution!® Book 030-0002: beCause, we will have Inspecting Generals, who go around Checking Up on those Working Soldiers, who will Remind them that if they do not Like some certain Swanky Fortress, there are 2 Million other Fortresses that they might Love; or, at least ONE of them, which they can Move into, for Free: beCause, all Transportation will be FREE of all Charges! (I gathered up all of those Butternut Squashes within just 2 Hours. Therefore, why should I make a Slave of myself, all Year Long, just to EAT? Why not have my own Garden, and take Good Care of it? Is that not most Practical and Reasonable? What are your Arguments Against it, O Lady Doubtfulness? †§‡)

05-08 [_] O Selected King, I Doubt that the Federal Government will Allow us to: "VOTE for The GOAT!" (The New Political Party that has Guaranteed Solutions for our Massive Problems!) By The Worldwide People's Revolution!® Book 109, whose Name will never be put on the Ballot for any Election: beCause, it would be a Great THREAT to the Evil Empire. †§‡

05-09 [_] Well, my Friend, "All of the Arguments are in Favor of our Selected King, who has Zero Challengers!" (Before you Attend another Election Deception, you should Carefully Study this Inspired Book with an Honest Open Mind!) By The Worldwide People's Revolution!® Book 085. Therefore, beCause your Selected King has Zero Challengers, he is Automatically the Elected KING of the Mountains, by what they call a Default in Computers. †§‡

05-10 [_] O Selected King, I will do my Best to Try to Discover some Crazy Person, who will Challenge you to that Office, who has a Better Master Plan than you have, who has Written more than 365 Inspired Books for us to Study, which Contain "Guaranteed Solutions!" (HOW to Solve our Local and Global Problems in the Most-Rational Manner Possible!) By The Worldwide People's Revolution!® Book 080. So, wish me Good Luck! May you LOSE! †§‡§§

— Chapter 06 —

Optional Workable Plans for Obtaining Worldwide Law, Order, Obedience, Peace and True Prosperity!

06-01 [_] Well, the First Thing that Naturally comes to my Mind is *the Mark of the Beast,* whereby each Person is given a Permanent Positive RFID (Radio Frequency Identification Number), whereby no one can Buy nor Sell anything without his or her NUMBERS: beCause those Numbers make it Possible for that Beastly FALSE Federal Government to have TOTAL CONTROL, with NO True Freedom, at all; but, they will use Orwellian Speech to make it Appear to be freedom! ‡

06-02 [_] So, O Selected King, it would not Actually be TRUE Prosperity, like you Propose; but, it would be another Kind of FALSE Prosperity, whereby the Masses of People would APPEAR to be Prosperous: beCause of having less Unemployment, less Black Market Drugs, and so on, until you get to Checking Out their Suicide Rates, Divorces, Wars, Taxes, Wounded Soldiers, Legal Drug Consumption, Murders, and all of the Evil Things that Fill Up Courthouse Record Books, at which Time you Discover that it is a FALSE Economic System, which everyone should HATE. However, the Brainwashed Children have been Tawt that we should not Hate anything: beCause, "Hate is Evil." "Hate is BAD," they say, and "Hate can Kill you!" However, if we Hated ALL that is EVIL, it might Save us from a lot of Needless Suffering! And one of those Evil Things would be that *Mark of the Beast,* which will give the False Government Total Control over all of us. †§‡

06-03 [_] Well, my Friend, if there is anything that People just Naturally HATE, it is Total Control.

How does democracy lead to tyranny?

Democracy then degenerates into **tyranny** where no one has discipline and society exists in chaos. **Democracy** is taken over by the longing for freedom. Power must be seized to maintain order. A champion will come along and experience power, which will **cause** him to become a tyrant.

en.wikipedia.org › wiki › Plato's_five_regimes
Plato's five regimes - Wikipedia

The **tyranny of the majority** (or **tyranny** of the masses) is an inherent weakness to **majority** rule in which the **majority** of an electorate pursues exclusively its own interests at the expense of those in the minority. ... Typical solutions, in this condition, are concurrent **majority** and supermajority rules.

en.wikipedia.org › wiki › Tyranny_of_the_majority
Tyranny of the majority - Wikipedia

What is the best type of government according to Aristotle?

Aristotle considers constitutional **government** (a combination of oligarchy and democracy under law) the ideal **form of government**, but he observes that none of the three are healthy and that states will cycle between the three **forms** in an abrupt and chaotic process known as the kyklos or anacyclosis.

en.wikipedia.org › wiki › Mixed_government
Mixed government - Wikipedia

Why does Plato not like democracy?

Plato rejected Athenian **democracy** on the basis that such **democracies** were anarchic societies without internal unity, that they followed citizens' impulses rather than pursuing the common good, that **democracies** are unable to allow a sufficient number of their citizens to have their voices heard, and that such ...

en.wikipedia.org › wiki › Criticism_of_democracy
Criticism of democracy - Wikipedia

Who is in charge of direct democracy?

In a **direct democracy**, which is also called pure **democracy** the decisions are not taken by representatives. All decisions are voted on by the people. When a budget or law needs to be passed, then the idea goes to the people. Large governments rarely make decisions this way.

simple.wikipedia.org › wiki › Direct_democracy
Direct democracy - Simple English Wikipedia, the free encyclopedia

(A Complete Master Plan for Solving the Countless Problems of Mankind!)

What are the three levels of government?

Government in the United States consists of **three** separate **levels**: the federal **government**, the state **governments**, and local **governments**.

doyle.house.gov › resources › about-our-government
About Our Government | Congressman Mike Doyle

Do we have the right to overthrow the government?

Right of revolution. In political philosophy, the **right** of revolution (or **right** of rebellion) is the **right** or duty of the people of a nation to **overthrow** a **government** that acts against their common interests and/or threatens the safety of the people without cause.

en.wikipedia.org › wiki › Right_of_revolution
Right of revolution - Wikipedia

What are the 3 types of democracy?

Consensus **democracy** – rule based on consensus rather than traditional majority rule. Constitutional **democracy** – governed by a constitution. Deliberative **democracy** – in which authentic deliberation, not only voting, is central to legitimate decision making.

en.wikipedia.org › wiki › Types_of_democracy
Types of democracy - Wikipedia

What is a true democracy?

Direct **democracy** or pure **democracy** is a form of **democracy** in which people decide on policy initiatives directly. This differs from the majority of currently established **democracies**, which are representative **democracies**.

en.wikipedia.org › wiki › Direct_democracy
Direct democracy - Wikipedia

What are the key elements of democracy?

According to American political scientist Larry Diamond, **democracy** consists of four **key elements**: a political system for choosing and replacing the government through free and fair elections; the active participation of the people, as citizens, in politics and civic life; protection of the human rights of all citizens; ...

en.wikipedia.org › wiki › Democracy
Democracy - Wikipedia

What makes the US a democracy?

Eugene Volokh of the UCLA School of Law notes that the **United States** exemplifies the varied nature of a constitutional republic—a country where some decisions (often local) are made by direct **democratic** processes, while others (often federal) are made by democratically elected representatives.

en.wikipedia.org › wiki › Democratic_republic
Democratic republic - Wikipedia

What is democracy in simple words?

A **democracy** means rule by the people. The name is used for different forms of government, where the people can take part in the decisions that affect the way their community is run. ... These leaders take this decision about laws. This is commonly called representative **democracy**. The process of choosing is called election.

simple.wikipedia.org › wiki › Democracy
Democracy - Simple English Wikipedia, the free encyclopedia

What Socrates said about democracy?

Plato's Republic presents a critical view of **democracy** through the narration of **Socrates**: "foolish leaders of **Democracy**, which is a charming form of government, full of variety and disorder, and dispensing a sort of equality to equals and unequaled alike." In his work, Plato lists 5 forms of government from best to ...

en.wikipedia.org › wiki › Criticism_of_democracy
Criticism of democracy - Wikipedia

What is the ideal form of government?

oligarchy: **government** by the few. timocracy: **government** by the honored or valued. tyranny: **government** by one for himself. aristocracy: **government** by the best (Plato's **ideal form of government**)

en.wikipedia.org › wiki › Mixed_government
Mixed government - Wikipedia

Aristotle was appointed as the head of the royal academy of Macedon. During **Aristotle's** time in the Macedonian court, he gave lessons not only to Alexander, but also to two other future kings: Ptolemy and Cassander.

en.wikipedia.org › wiki › Aristotle
Aristotle - Wikipedia

What did democracy really mean in Athens?

Greek **democracy** created at **Athens** was direct, rather than representative: any adult male citizen over the age of 20 could take part, and it was a duty to do so. The officials of the **democracy** were in part elected by the Assembly and in large part chosen by lottery in a process called sortition.

en.wikipedia.org › wiki › Athenian_democracy
Athenian democracy - Wikipedia

Formation of **Political Parties**. **Political** factions or **parties** began to **form** during the struggle over ratification of the federal Constitution of 1787. Friction between them increased as attention shifted from the creation of a new federal government to the question of how powerful that federal government would be.

www.loc.gov › exhibits › formation-of-political-parties
Formation of Political Parties - Creating the United States ...

Tyrant. Tyrant, **Greek** tyrannos, a cruel and oppressive ruler or, in ancient **Greece**, a ruler who seized **power** unconstitutionally or inherited such **power**. ... Thus, the opportunity arose for ambitious men to seize **power** in the name of the oppressed.

www.britannica.com › topic › tyrant
tyrant | Definition & Facts | Britannica

These people may be distinguished by nobility, wealth, education, corporate, religious, political, or military control. Such states are often controlled by families who pass their influence from one generation to the next, but inheritance is not a necessary condition of **oligarchy**.

en.wikipedia.org › wiki › Oligarchy
Oligarchy - Wikipedia

What is known about oligarchy in ancient Greece?

The coup overthrew the democratic government of **ancient** Athens and replaced it with a short-lived **oligarchy known** as the Four Hundred. ... The movement toward **oligarchy** was led by a number of prominent and wealthy Athenians, who held positions of power in the Athenian army at Samos in coordination with Alcibiades.

en.wikipedia.org › wiki › Athenian_coup_of_411_BC
Athenian coup of 411 BC - Wikipedia

What was life like in Sparta?

The fears of outside invasion and of a helot revolt led **Sparta** to create a dominant
military culture that affected all aspects of Spartan **life**. Because **Sparta** based its
power on military strength, **Spartans** spent little time focusing on arts and culture. From
birth, Spartan citizens were raised to become soldiers. Aug 21, 2015

www.cpsk12.org › cms › lib8 › Centricity › Domain
Life in Ancient Sparta

What event killed the most humans?

Wars and armed conflicts with highest estimated death tolls of 100,000 or more

Event	Lowest estimate	Location
World War II	60,000,000	Worldwide
Three Kingdoms	36,000,000	China
Mongol conquests	30,000,000	Eurasia
European colonization of the Americas	8,400,000	Americas

48 more rows

en.wikipedia.org › wiki › List_of_wars_and_anthropogen...
List of wars and anthropogenic disasters by death toll - Wikipedia

Who was the most hated king?

King John I may forever be known as a Bad **King** following that seminal history
textbook 1066 and All That, but according to history authors, it is Henry VIII who should
bear the title of the worst monarch in history. Sep 2, 2015

www.theguardian.com › books › sep › henry-viii-voted-...
Henry VIII voted worst monarch in history | Books | The Guardian

Who was the craziest king in history?

Caligula, Emperor of Rome (A.D. 12-41)

Topping even his nephew Nero for the crown of cruelest and **craziest** Roman emperor,
Caligula was known for his lavish projects, his sadism and his eccentricity. Nov 4, 2014

www.history.com › news › 10-allegedly-mad-monarchs
10 (Allegedly) Mad Monarchs - HISTORY

Who was the most feared person in history?

The 25 most ruthless leaders of all time

- Qin Shi Huang. Britannica. ...
- Gaius Julius Caesar Augustus Germanicus (aka Caligula) Wikipedia. ...
- Attila the Hun. Wikimedia. ...
- Wu Zetian. Wikimedia. ...
- Genghis Khan. ...
- Tomas de Torquemada. ...
- Timur (aka Tamerlane) ...
- Vlad III, Prince of Wallachia (aka Vlad Drăculea or Vlad the Impaler)

More items... • Oct 7, 2015

www.businessinsider.com › most-ruthless-leaders-of-all-ti...

Most ruthless leaders of all time - Business Insider

Who won the Persian War?

Greeks

The **Greeks** won a decisive victory, losing only 192 men to the Persians' 6,400 (according to the historian Herodotus). May 8, 2020

www.britannica.com › event › Greco-Persian-Wars

Greco-Persian Wars | Definition, Summary, Facts, Effects, & History

Sparta was a warrior **society** in ancient Greece that reached the height of its power after defeating rival city-state Athens in the Peloponnesian War (431-404 B.C.). **Spartan** culture **was** centered on loyalty to the state and **military** service. Nov 12, 2009

www.history.com › topics › ancient-history › sparta

Sparta, Ancient Greece: Military, Women & Facts - HISTORY

Is United States a plutocracy?

According to Kevin Phillips, author and political strategist to Richard Nixon, the **United States** is a **plutocracy** in which there is a "fusion of money and government."

en.wikipedia.org › wiki › Plutocracy

Plutocracy - Wikipedia

Is United States an oligarchy?

The modern **United States** has also been described as an **oligarchy** because economic elites and organized groups representing special interests have substantial independent impacts on U.S. government policy, while average citizens and mass-based interest groups have little or no independent influence.

en.wikipedia.org › wiki › Oligarchy

Oligarchy - Wikipedia

Which is the largest democracy country in the world?

India (Hindi: Bhārat), officially the **Republic of India** (Hindi: Bhārat Gaṇarājya), is a country in South Asia. It is the seventh-largest country by area, the second-most populous country, and the most populous democracy in the world.

en.wikipedia.org › wiki › India

India - Wikipedia

06-04 [_] So, there we have it from Mr. Google — India is the Largest DUMBmocracy in the World, which Suffers with hundreds of millions of Extremely Poor People, in spite of having huge Mountains of Rocks to Work with, whereby each Family could be Living in one of those "Beautiful Swanky Stone Dome Home COMPLEXES!" (HOW to Build SECURE Tax-proof, Insurance-proof, Self-air-conditioned, Paint-proof, Rot-proof, Termite-proof, Mouse-proof, Fireproof, Tornado-proof, Hurricane-proof, Thief-proof, and BOMB-PROOF Houses!) By The Worldwide People's Revolution!® Book 102, if they had a Righteous King to Govern them; but, like the Haitian and American Dupes, they do not Believe in KINGS, at all! Therefore, they have Suffered for hundreds of Years under the Tyranny of Extreme POVERTY!‡

06-05 [_] O Selected King, we just Learned that ALL Forms of Government are BAD, and the Worst Kind is the one that Manages to Deceive most of the People by Means of Election Deceptions, who Vainly Imagine that they are Free with a Capital F, just beCause they are not Locked Up in Prisons; but, they are Actually Education Slaves, Work Slaves, Tax Slaves, Interest Slaves, Insurance Slaves, Mortgage Slaves, Credit Card Debt Slaves, and Endless Bills SLAVES!

06-06 [_] Well, my Friend, the Economic System that I Propose has NO SLAVES AT ALL; but, everyone who Joins it simply Volunteers to Do at least 4 Hours of Common Skilled Labor per Workday, or the

Equivalent thereof, just to Cover all of the Costs of Living within "Beautiful Swanky PALACES!" (A New Concept in Living Habits — Swanky Palaces for Poor People!) By The Worldwide People's Revolution!® Book 066, which will Require about 6 Years of Work, just to get all of them Built for 7 Billion People, IF they Want them, who will have to "VOTE for The GOAT!" (The New Political Party that has Guaranteed Solutions for our Massive Problems!) By The Worldwide People's Revolution!® Book 109, just to get them: beCause, that Scapegoat can be Blamed for whatever goes WRong, after he is put in Charge. †§‡

06-07 |_| So, O Selected King, in the TYRANNICAL SWANGKEENOMIKS System that you Propose, each of those "GLORIOUS Swanky Hotels Castles and Fortresses!" (Beautiful Planned City States for WISE Intelligent Well-Educated People with Common Sense and Good Understanding!) By The Worldwide People's Revolution!® Book 019B, will Govern itself, according to their own Elected Laws and Flexible Rules, whereby they can all be Happy with themselves: beCause, they will all be Free to Do that, considering the Fact that they are all Intelligent Well-Educated People, who only Need to HEAR the Options to Choose from, and make up their own Minds, after their Disputes: beCause it is Assumed that they are NOT Stupid! †§‡§§

06-08 |_| ♦♦ O Selected King, if I Understand it Correctly, "The New RIGHTEOUS One-World Government!" will Furnish all of the Money, Tools, and Materials for Constructing at least 2 Million of those "GLORIOUS Swanky Hotels Castles and Fortresses!" which will eventually be in the Total Control of their own Elected Officials, who may Choose whatever Form of Government that they Like, after they have Filled Out and Filed: "The Complete SURVEYS of our VALUES!" (SURVEYS of Religious Spiritual Political Governmental Sexual Social Moral Economical Business Labor Habitual and Miscellaneous VALUES!) By The Worldwide People's Revolution!® Book 059, whereby Government Computers can easily Determine WHERE each Person Belongs with other People of Like-mindedness: so that People, who are Like Sheeps and Goats, are not being taken Advantage of by People who are Like Lions nor Wolves. In other Words, Like-minded People should Liv TOGETHER, whereby they can all Liv in PEACE. For Example, if the White Supremists do not Want to Liv with any Black People, they will not have to; but, if they Want to Liv with them, they can Check the Appropriate Boxes.‡

06-09 [_] Well, my Friend, can you Think of a Better Plan, than that, for Obtaining Peace among all Races of Peoples of all Colors, who will be Assisted by **"The New RIGHTEOUS One-World Government!"** to Build their own Beautiful Planned City States, who may Accept or Reject the Help of that Good RIGHTEOUS Government: beCause, they will also be Free to Accept or Reject it; or, not even Join **"The New RIGHTEOUS One-World Government!"** whereby they can Remain in their Present-day Cities of Confusion, if they Want to: beCause, no one is going to FORCE anyone to Say nor Do what is RIIT. In Fact, they are Welcome to Liv in Swamps, Jungles, Deserts, Mountains, or wherever they Like it: beCause, that is what True Freedom is all about! §‡

06-10 [_] O Selected King, I will Bet that those Lying Conniving Edomites will figure out HOW to take Advantages of us Poor People, and make us into their Slaves, no matter what Happens. †§‡

{6-year-old Lupe has the Bull Whip in Hand to Manage her Slaves Properly!}

— Chapter 07 —

Guaranteed Protection
for the Poor People!

07-01 [_] WOW! How in the World, O Selected King, could "The New RIGHTEOUS One-World Government!" Protect ALL of the Poor People, Worldwide? What Kind of a Police State would that be? How many Members of that Wicked Government will have to become Policemen and Security Guards, just to Watch over all of those Potential Capitalist and Communist Criminals?

07-02 [_] Well, my Friend, I am only Referring to the Wise Poor People, who Join "The New RIGHTEOUS One-World Government!" and particularly the "Seven Great Armies of Working Soldiers!" (HOW to Provide a Way for Everyone to WORK: so as to Eliminate Poverty, Crimes, Drug Abuses, Prisons and Unnecessary Taxes!) By The Worldwide People's Revolution!® Book 015B, who will be Managed by that Good Government, whereby each Army will have its Responsibilities, which are Explained within that Inspired Book, who will be Assisted by "The Swanky Associations of Working Soldiers!" (A Fascinating Collection of Various Kinds of Voluntary Working Soldiers!) By The Worldwide People's Revolution!® Book 018B, until all of the Swanky Hotels and Fortresses are Finished, and then those Seven Armies will no longer be Needed: beCause, "The Swanky Associations of Working Soldiers!" will Manage the Building of Swanky Castles, the Transportation Systems, the Telephone System, the Television Networks and Radio Stations for "The New RIGHTEOUS One-World Government!" which will be in all Major Languages, Worldwide, which will also have its own Internet System: beCause no Hackers will be Able to Hack into it, nor even get online with it: beCause, it will be a Closed System, which will only Work with Government-produced Computers and whatever is Required for making it Function Correctly for Righteous People, who Agree. †§‡

07-03 [_] There is a Picture of Tripoli, Lebanon, which is just another Typical Capitalist Economic Disaster: beCause none of those Extremely Poor People have any All-Mineral Organic Gardens to Feed themselves: beCause, they Bought into the American Capitalist Pack of Edomite Lies. For Example, a Box of Cheerio Cereal is 20 Dollars for one Pound (0.453 Kilograms), and Wages are like 5 Dollars per Hour, if you can Find a Job. Most of them cannot. Therefore, how are they supposed to Feed their Children? The entire Lifestyle is INSANE! In Fact, if a Crazy King had Ordered those People to Build such Trashy Capitalist Apartment Houses for themselves to Liv in, they would have Rebelled, and told him to go straight to Hell: beCause of the Insanity of it all. †§‡

07-04 [_] So, O Selected King of **"The New RIGHTEOUS One-World Government!"** if you had been in Charge of the Whole World, you would not have Allowed such an Evil Thing to Happen, right? You would have never Permitted those People to be Mistreated like that, right? §‡

07-05 [_] Well, my Friend, first of all, it is very Unlikely that I will ever get Elected to be the King of the WHOLE World, when I will be very "Lucky" to be the Elected King of "The New RIGHTEOUS One-World Government!" which will not be Interfering with any Established National Governments, at all: beCause, "The New RIGHTEOUS One-World Government!" will only be Concerned with whatever is going on within those "GLORIOUS Swanky Hotels Castles and Fortresses!" which will be City States within States and Nations. For Example, let us say that you are a Healthy Young Man, who Needs a Good Job with Extremely Good Wages; but, you hardly know how to Reed Werdz. Therefore, you Visit the nearest Swanky Recruiting Station, which Discovers what you Believe: beCause, they Issue a Copy of "The Complete SURVEYS of our VALUES!" (SURVEYS of Religious Spiritual Political Governmental Sexual Social Moral Economical Business Labor Habitual and Miscellaneous VALUES!) By The Worldwide People's Revolution!® Book 059, to you and to whomever else Wants to Join, who may have to Help you to Reed it and Check the Boxes with Statements that you Agree with, with the Correct Colors of INK — as in, RED for Disagree, and GREEN for Agree, which may take a few Days, if you are Slow. However, it is no Big Problem: beCause that Recruiting Station will be a Normal Hotel, which has lots of Beds, Meals, and whatever you Need to be Comfortable.

07-06 [_] So, O Selected King, let us say that I am 18 Years Old, and as Horny as an Old Goat, and have never done so much as one Day of Work during my entire Life, and do not even know how to Clean my own Feets — will there be someone at the Recruiting Station to Help me, or not?

07-07 [_] Well, my Friend, it will be Assumed that no one Knows how Best to Wash their Feets, nor anything else; and some of them will probably have Athlete's Foot Disease when they show up, as well as Lice, Sex Diseases, Colds, Flus, or whatever, who will have to be Sent to a **Lost Creature's Hotel** with some Medics to Help them, which Hotels will not be Located within any Cities; but, on some Farms, which will have Gardens and Kitchens to Work in, along with Teachers and Instructors, if they can be Found, and if the System is not FLOODED with far too many Recruits, at once. In other Words, we Hope that only a few Recruits will show up, each Day, and that some of them will Know how to Do something, who can Help Teach the others, whereby they will not Starve to Death, who will have to Change their Diets; but, if they are Hungry, those Avocado-Potato Salads will Taste Really GOOD and Satisfying. Moreover, after they get themselves Organized, and finally Produce Extra Foods, some of those Foods will be Shipped to those City Hotels for the New Recruits, who can Eat those Foods for Free: beCause it will not be long before they will Complete **"The Complete SURVEYS of our VALUES!" (SURVEYS of Religious Spiritual Political Governmental Sexual Social Moral Economical Business Labor Habitual and Miscellaneous VALUES!) By The Worldwide People's Revolution!®** Book 059, whereby the Computers can Discover the Best Places for them to be Shipped to, in Order to Begin their New Lives, even if it is far away, in another Country: beCause they will get to Liv with Like-minded People, which alone will make them very Happy for it: beCause of not knowing that any such People Existed before their Discovery. Therefore, be Sure to be Perfectly Honest about your Answers to the Surveys' Questions, and Ask for Help, if there is any Doubt about something. †§‡

07-08 [_] O Selected King, it will Prove to be Interesting concerning just how all of that Works out, and WHO will Qualify to Manage any such Recruiting Stations, and Spoiled Brats, who will not know how to Do much of anything, except to Play with their Balls and Tally Whackers, who will have to go through a Basic-Training Camp for 6 Months, or more, just to get Properly Educated about how to Feed themselves, whereby they might Qualify to Teach other Recruits. †§‡

07-09 [_] Well, my Friend, Obtaining Qualified Teachers will be a Major Problem: beCause all such Teachers are already Employed in Colleges and Universities, if not in **"The Public School of IGNERUNT FQLZ!" (HOW we have been GRAATLEE DISEEVD by Capitalism!) By The Worldwide People's Revolution!®** Book 024B. Therefore, it might Require us to DRAFT them into those **"Seven Great Armies of**

Working Soldiers!" (HOW to Provide a Way for Everyone to WORK: so as to Eliminate Poverty, Crimes, Drug Abuses, Prisons and Unnecessary Taxes!) By The Worldwide People's Revolution!® Book 015B, with the Kind Permission of all Federal Governments, Worldwide, until we get the System Working Correctly, which will Naturally Cause many of those Recruits to REBEL; but, they should be Thankful that they are not being Drafted into an Army of Murderous Soldiers, whereby they might be Sent to some Hateful Gory War, to be Wounded, Killed or Maimed. After all, if we do have to Draft Working Soldiers, they will Naturally get the Worst of the Jobs to Attend to: beCause of being Rebels. Therefore, in Order to AVOID all of that Nonsense, we must Conduct "The GREAT Worldwide TELEVISED Court HEARING!" (That Great Meeting of the Most-Intelligent and Well-Educated Minds!) By The Worldwide People's Revolution!® Book 041B, and Persuade the Masses of People that it is in their Greatest Benevolent Interest to Cooperate with my Plan, which was Revealed to me by the Great Creator God, himself, and Work Together with Cooperation and LOVE: beCause there are Ways for God to Soften their Hearts, and Straighten them Out, the Hard Way, by Droughts, Famines, Sicknesses, Diseases, Wars, PLAGUES, and whatever else is Good. {See: "What will you Do when the Rain STOPS?" (God's Last Resort to Save Mankind from his MADNESS!) By The Worldwide People's Revolution!® B-101!}§

07-10 |_| O Selected King, most of us Americans have no Idea what we would Do, if the Rain should STOP: beCause we do not Know HOW to Liv in Deserts. Nevertheless, I am Wondering just HOW we are going to have Guaranteed Protection for the Poor People, who are likely to be Multiplied by the Billions, if we Fail to get those **"GLORIOUS Swanky Hotels Castles and Fortresses!" (Beautiful Planned City States for WISE Intelligent Well-Educated People with Common Sense and Good Understanding!) By The Worldwide People's Revolution!®** Book 019B, Constructed. Therefore, I Suggest that we should Act WISELY, and DEMAND that Great Meeting of the Most-Intelligent and Well-Educated Minds, just to Discover that they can easily be Persuaded to Construct those Beautiful Planned City States, and especially if they have some Big Beautiful Muscles: beCause there is a very Good Chance that they will easily be Persuaded to get on with it, and that will Protect all of the Poor People. Otherwise, they can Look Forward to HELL ON EARTH: beCause, that is all that Capitalism, Socialism, and Communism have to Offer! †§‡

— Chapter 08 —

The Songs of the Mockingbirds

08-01 [_] O Selected King, it looks to me like you have gotten yourself into a Real Swanky Pickle Barrel, with no Way Out of it: beCause, it will Require a Trillion Dollars, just to Build those **Lost Creatures' Hotels,** out around all of these Cities of Confusion, and to Feed and Juice Up those Poor Ignorant Children, who will be coming to those Recruiting Stations, by the Millions, looking for 60 Dollars per Hour for Setting Marble Tiles on the Solid Stone Walls of Swanky Hotels for Visitors, which are bound to be Disasters: beCause of Unskilled Working Soldiers, who never did anything Constructive during their entire Lives — let alone, something so Precise as Tile-setting, which will Require no less than 6 Months of Practice, just to get them Straight, and in Line! †§‡§§

08-02 [_] ♦♦ Well, my Friend, before anyone will get to Touch those Beautiful Marble Tiles, they will first of all have to Learn how to Set Ceramic Tiles Properly, on the Solid Concrete Walls of those Large Swanky Cisterns, each of which will Cost about 2-Million Dollars, just for Materials: beCause of Containing about 500,000 Gallons of Fresh

Living Water, which we will have to Import from Mount Zion, from the Mighty Jordan River, which Surrounds it, which Runs Out of the Hole in the Far North, from the Hollow Earth, which you have most likely never Heard of; but, it is for Real, or else *Psalm 48* is nothing but Jewish Mythology! Nevertheless, as for being in a Pickle Barrel for a Lack of Money, that would be no Problem, at all, if I could get Paid a Fair Amount for my Inspired Books: beCause, right now, a 45-dollar Book gets me only $1.25, while it gains Amazonico about 40 Dollars, and the Remaining Money is for Shipping and Handling. However, if there were any True Justice, I would be getting the 40 Dollars, and Amazonico would be getting $1.25: beCause they have Millions of Books to Sell, and Jeff Bezos is already a Multi-Billionaire, who could also Share some of his Billions of Dollars to Help us to Build the First Lost Creature's Hotel, if he were Sincerely Concerned for the Welfare of Mankind: beCause there are no less than 2 Billion Poor Young People, who Desperately Need some Survival Skills, which they can Learn, while Working at those **Lost Creatures' Hotels,** which will have about 100 Acres of All-Mineral Organic Gardens to Attend to, while Learning those Survival Skills, who will Naturally make a lot of Mistakes; but, those will be Schools for them, and their Teachers — none of whom would be Paid anything: beCause, it will Require at least 4 Hours of Common Skilled Labor, just to Cover all of their Expenses — such as Foods, Clothing, Rooms, Showers, Classrooms, Tools, Televisions, and whatever they have to Work with, which will be like a Common Military Sacrifice, until they get to Move into their own "Beautiful Swanky Stone Dome Home COMPLEXES!" (HOW to Build SECURE Tax-proof, Insurance-proof, Self-air-conditioned, Paint-proof, Rot-proof, Termite-proof, Mouse-proof, Fireproof, Tornado-proof, Hurricane-proof, Thief-proof, and BOMB-PROOF Houses!) By The Worldwide People's Revolution!® Book 102, when they will just Automatically become Moderately RICH!

08-03 [_] O Selected King of the Ignorant Fools, it will just Naturally Require TRAINLOADS of Rocks for Building those Swanky Hotels, which Means that you will Need to Build Railroads for Transporting the Rocks from the Mountains to the Valleys, wherever those "GLORIOUS Swanky Hotels Castles and Fortresses!" will be Built. After all, you must Remember that it Required 7 Years for you to Build that Tiny Swanky Cistern, which holds only 100,000 Gallons of Contaminated Spring Water, which has Tree Leaves falling into it, which might be Good for Watering those All-Mineral Organic Gardens; but, it is not Drinkable Water, as it should be for Proper Survival. {See: "The LUSCIOUS All-Mineral Organic Method of Gardening!" (HOW to Grow DELICIOUS Satisfying Foods for Potential Kingz and Kweenz in Beautiful Swanky PALACES!) By The Worldwide People's Revolution!® Book 021B, for the DETAILS.} †§‡§§

08-04 |_| Well, my Friend, it took me 2 Years, just to Build that Developed Spring Water House; and there is more Work under the Ground, than above it. It also Serves as a Drying House for Bags of Sweet Potatoes, which are Hung from the Ceiling in 2 Rows, which can Dry 2 Tons at a Time from the nearby 5-Acre All-Mineral Organic Garden, which has a Water Outlet every 100-feet in all Directions, just to make Sure that all of the Plants can get Watered from the Spring House, which puts out 50,000 Gallons of Water per Day, if it is Needed, which Garden could easily Feed 100 Working Soldiers, if it were Managed Correctly, which would also Require a Walk-in Root Cellar, Walk-in Cooler, and Walk-in Freezer for KALE: beCause, that same 5-Acre Garden can Grow 40 Tons of Kale, each Autumn, which are Extremely GOOD-Tasting Greens, which should be Eaten with Fresh Green Onions, and a little Avocado Oil on the Steamed Kale, along with some San-J Tamari Sauce, which is a Royal Feast for Kings and Queens in "Beautiful Swanky PALACES!" (A New Concept in Living Habits — Swanky Palaces for Poor People!) By The Worldwide People's Revolution!® Book 066. However, if you Doubt it, it is only beCause you have not Experienced it with a Swanky Sweet Potato, which has been Thoroughly and Slowly Baked in a Brick or Stone Oven, like the one that I Built at Frog Level, near Central, Arkansas, which I did not get to Finished: beCause of being Pressed with other, more-urgent Matters: beCause of being a One-Man Army, you might say, who Needed a hundred Young Workers. †§‡

08-05 |_| O Selected King of "The New RIGHTEOUS One-World Government!" your Delicious Green Onions are so GOOD that even the Queen of England would Love them, in spite of the Fact that she does not Like to Eat Onions, nor Garlic; but, that is only beCause she has never Tasted of your Most-Delicious Onions, which are so Sweet and Mild that they can be Eaten alone; but, I Like them with Home-grown Organic Popcorn, whereby just 4 of those Onions and a Bowl of Popcorn makes a Good Satisfying Meal for a Young Working Soldier, with just a little of that San-J Tamari Sauce and some Virgin Olive Oil, which makes another Royal Feast, if you are Plenty Hungry, after Digging Up those Potatoes from the All-Mineral Organic Swanky Garden. ‡

08-06 [_] Well, my Friend, that Picture shows our Special Swanky Garden, just before we finished Sifting the Rocks Out of 18,000 Wheelbarrows of Dirt, which was one-third Rocks. We Saved the Sifted Dirt behind Solid DOUBLE Concrete Walls, which left a Chicken-run and Dog-run between the Walls. The Chickens kept out the Bugs during the Daytime, and the Dogs kept out the Raccoons and Opossums at Night; but, in order to keep the Crows out of the Sweet Corn, we Tied Fishing Lines between the Red Steel Posts, in both Directions, which formed an Invisible NETWORK, which Spooked the Devil out of those Crows when they Swooped Down, and Touched those Fishing Lines! Therefore, they soon told the other Crows to Avoid our Special Garden: beCause of being a TRAP for Crows! Therefore, in 20 Years, we never Lost one Cob of Corn to the Crows!

08-07 [_] However, right next-door to us, just across the Barbed-wire Fence, the Hog-farming Naaber spread out 4,000 Tons of Hog Manure, 6-inches deep, to Pollute the Land, Water and Air, which the EPA (Environmental PROTECTION Agency) would not even Look at, let alone Smell of it: beCause, they were Stationed 150 Miles away, in Little Rock, Arkansas, who were Underfunded, and far too Poor to Inspect a thousand or more of those Hog Farms. In Fact, they were the Unholy Ones, who Ordered that Poor Capitalist Farmer to CLEAN OUT his Hog Manure Pond, who had no Idea that we Lived right next-door, and might Want some Fresh Air to Breathe.

08-08 [_] O Selected King, when you are Elected to be the RIGHTEOUS KING of **"The New RIGHTEOUS One-World Government!"** you will be Able to Relate with those Millions of Poor People, who Liv not far from Industrial Hog Farms, Chicken Factories, and Cattle Feed Lots, where the Cattle are Wading around in their own Manure, up to their Bellies, when they should be Free in Open Fields. {See: **"The Process of Making a RIGHTEOUS KING!" (A Fascinating Autobiography of our Selected King!) By The Worldwide People's Revolution!®** Book 082.}

08-09 [_] Well, my Friend, that Poor Ignorant Hog Farmer had no Idea what Wonderful Fragrant Mangos can be Grown with just a little of that Hog Manure: beCause those Mango Trees have a Unique Way of Transforming that Odious Stink into Sweet Fragrance, when the Manure is Properly Composted and Placed under "Profitable Swanky MULCHING ROCKS!" (30 Advantages for Using Swanky Mulching Rocks in an All-Mineral Organic Garden!) By The Worldwide People's Revolution!® Book 098, which have more than 40 Advantages that "The Public School of IGNERUNT FQLZ!" (HOW we have been GRAATLEE DISEEVD by Capitalism!) By The Worldwide People's Revolution!® Book 024B, never even Mentioned! In Fact, they have most likely never Heard about those Profitable Mulching Rocks: beCause, the Billionaire DEPARTment of Agriculture never even Heard of them. However, even if they were Hog-tied on a Bed in the middle of that Hog Manure that was Spread Out on the Hog Farm, for a whole Month, they would still say: "We Americans could never Afford those Swanky Mulching Rocks: beCause, we Tax Slaves are already 140 Trillion Dollars in Debt to the Devil. Therefore, where would we get 280 Dollars for Buying just ONE Granite Rock, which is 2 feet square, one-inch thick, and one inch Cut Off of each Corner, which makes a Perfect Place for Planting Bell Peppers, Hot Peppers, Fennel, Mustard, Cucumbers, Tomatoes, Okra, Cantaloupes, Watermelons, Cabbages, Broccoli, Cauliflowers, Squashes of all Kinds, Blackberries, Raspberries, Blueberries, Gooseberries, Currents, Grapes, Flowers of Various Kinds, and whatever might Want a Consistent Supply of Moisture for Growing Well." Indeed, the Secretary of

Agriculture would say, "We are Poor Capitalists, who cannot Afford to Do anything Correctly: beCause, we do not have a Loving, RIGHTEOUS, Compassionate, Godly Government." And I would have to Agree with him. †§‡§§

08-10 [_] O Selected King of "The New RIGHTEOUS One-World Government!" what you Need most is some COOPERATION by the Masses of Extremely Poor Education Slaves, Work Slaves, Tax Slaves, Insurance Slaves, Rent Slaves, Home-owner Slaves, Interest Slaves, Mortgage Slaves, ElecTrickery Bills Slaves, Food Bills Slaves, Water Bills Slaves, Gas Bills Slaves, Telephone Bills Slaves, Internet Bills Slaves, Entertainment Bills Slaves, Transportation Bills Slaves, Repair Bills Slaves, Drug Bills Slaves, Doctor Bills Slaves, Hospital Bills Slaves, Childcare Bills Slaves, Nursing Home Bills Slaves, and Funeral Home Bills Slaves, who Want to be LIBERATED from the Prison of

Lies — who Want to be Set Up Properly on the Land, just to Feed themselves Correctly. After all, why Pay 3 Dollars for a single Ripe Mango, when the Tree is only 8 Dollars, and might eventually Bear 10,000 Delicious Mangos, for 100 Years to Come!?‡

08-11 [_] Well, my Friend, one of those Mango Trees can get 40 feet Tall, and Require a Crane with a Box, just to Harvest those 10,000 Mangos, which no Poor Person could ever Afford: beCause one of those Crane Trucks Costs about 600,000 Dollars. However, a Swanky Army of Working Soldiers could easily Afford to Buy as many as they might Need for Harvesting Trillions of Mangos, all around the World: beCause of having "The New RIGHTEOUS One-World Government!" which would have an Unlimited Supply of Good Money, which would have to be EARNED by Honest Labor, without any Loans, without any Interest / Usury, and without any Taxes: beCause, all of the People have Agreed to Learn, Believe, Love and OBEY: **"The New MAGNIFIED Version of the 20 Commandments,"** which anyone with any Brains can Discover in: **"LIGHTNING STRIKES Versus Lightning Bugs!" (HOW you can Become Moderately RICH, without Telling any Lies nor Selling any Trash!) By The Worldwide People's Revolution!®** Book 074, which the Federal Government could put into every American Mailbox.

08-12 [_] O Selected King of "Provable Truths that True Christians cannot Rightly Deny!" (A Fair Challenge for all Professing "Christians" to Meditate on with Honest Open Minds!) By The Worldwide People's Revolution!® Book 086, any Rich Church could also put a Copy of Book 074 into every American Mailbox, if they were not Spiritual COWARDS! After all, you can Order them from Amazon at BULK RATES for only 6 Dollars per Book, which the Church of Jesus Christ of Latter-day Sinners could Distribute Wisely in all Mormon Mailboxes, just to get this Forest Fire of Truths Burning! Indeed, they have BILLIONS of Dollars, just for Doing that, if they will, whereby they might get "A New Jerusalem in the Great State of Flexible Texas!" (HOW to make Good Use of the Mississippi River!) By The Worldwide People's Revolution!® Book 090, Constructed, for FREE: beCause of what is Written in, "The New MAGNIFIED Version of The Book of MORMON!" (The Story of the White and Dark Indians in the Americas!) By Big Chief Standsover Bull in River of Life! Book 040, which is a Real COMEDY, you might say; but, it is as Subtle as a Snake, which will Plant Good Seeds of Provable Truths within the Hearts and Minds of whomever Studies it, which only Appears to be Anti-Mormon, when it is Actually Promoting the Great Truths that are Tawt by that Church. †§‡§§

08-13 [_] Well, my Friend, Book 090 is a Companion Book of: "The Great World TEMPLE of PEACE!" (The Glory of Jerusalem Arises Again in the Great State of Flexible Texas!) By The Worldwide

People's Revolution!® Book 017B, which the Mormons could Manage, if the Jews are not Interested in it: beCause of being Distracted from Spiritual Things by their "DIETS!" (A Reasonable Solution for the "Eternal Controversy"!) By The Worldwide People's Revolution!® Book 037, whereby many of them have become as Fat as HOGS, in spite of the Fact that the Book of Mormon says: *"Come you Out from among the Wicked Ones, and be you Separated from them, says the Supreme Ruler, and Touch NONE of their Unclean Things,"* which would Naturally Include those Stinking, Noisy, Polluting Abominations, called: CARS, which are not Needed within **"A New Jerusalem in the Great State of Flexible Texas!"** (HOW to make Good Use of the Mississippi River!) By The Worldwide People's Revolution!® Book 090. †§‡

08-14 [ ] O Selected King of "The Worldwide People's Revolution!" (A Comprehensive Plan for Obtaining Worldwide Law, Order, Obedience, Peace and True Prosperity!) By The Worldwide People's Revolution!® Book 108, I can see your Camper Van and your Brother Vern at the far-right side of that Picture, which is Proof that you are just another HYPOCRITE: beCause you are also Polluting God's Air, Water, and Land with your own Abomination! Yes, you should be Careful how you Judge the Mormons, who are Latter-day SAINTS: beCause, *"... with whatever Judgment that you Use to Condemn other People, you shall also be Judged and Condemned." — The Drunken Jesus, who is known as the Winebibber and Glutton.* Indeed, none of those Saints would Condemn you for Driving a Stinking Polluting Camper Van: beCause, they also do the same thing with their own Cars, Pickup Trucks, SUV's, and Mobile Homes: beCause they also Like to Visit the National Parks, which are especially Beautiful in Utah, which is the Wonderland of American National Parks, which everyone in the Whole World should get to See for themselves.§

08-15 [_] Well, my Friend, I am not Condemning anyone for Driving a Car, nor for Polluting the Environment: beCause I gave up Driving, and only use the Elevators, Escalators, and Electric Subway Trains: beCause I WALK with Jesus Christ and Saint Paul, which does not Bother my Conscience even the Slightest Bit. Therefore, my Habits have Changed a lot during the past 20 Years, which is Proof that we could all Change, and take up New Habits, and even Save our World from the Persistent MADNESS of "The Nature of CAPITALISM!" (A List of the EVILS of CAPITALISM!) By The Worldwide People's Revolution!® Book 038. Indeed, that is the Primary Reason for Building those "GLORIOUS Swanky Hotels Castles and Fortresses!" (Beautiful Planned City States for WISE Intelligent Well-Educated People with Common Sense and Good Understanding!) By The Worldwide People's Revolution!® Book 019B. †§‡

08-16 [_] O American Rebels of Reason and Logic, "All of the Arguments are in Favor of our Selected King, who has Zero Challengers!" (Before you Attend another Election Deception, you should Carefully Study this Inspired Book with an Honest Open Mind!) By The Worldwide People's Revolution!® Book 085. After all, who can Rightly Argue that there is something GOOD about Trillions of Tons of Capitalist TRASH, since NONE of it is Needed nor Wanted within those "Beautiful Swanky PALACES!" (A New Concept in Living Habits — Swanky Palaces for Poor People!) By The Worldwide People's Revolution!® Book 066? †§‡

08-17 [_] Well, my Friend, that is what I have been Publishing for more than 40 Years; but, it seems that the Belgiculture People are the only ones who have Ears that can Hear! Perhaps they have enough Fresh Air for their Brains to Function Riit? Maybe they even Like Home-grown Pickled Beets, made with Montana Clover Honey, Apple Cider Vinegar, and Mustard Seeds? †§‡

08-18 [_] O Selected King of the Mountains, how Beautiful are the Feet of those Wise People, who Stand upon the Glorious Mountains to Publish Peace! I would Think that it would be the Duty of every Church in the Whole World to put a Copy of this Inspired Book in every

Mailbox, in an Organized Way, by United Effort, whereby no Mailbox has 2 Copies; but, only one: beCause of Discovering the Postal Service, which can Distribute the Books Properly: beCause that is what it was Established for. Therefore, they have Bulk Rates on their Mail — such as 6 Cents per Letter, or 30 Cents per Book, which Amazon could put in Plastic Wrappers, except that they would only Pollute the World that much more. Therefore, they should be Wrapped in plain Brown Paper. †§‡

08-19 [_] Well, my Friend, we already Know for a Fact that all of the Soldiers in this World of Wonders can Read and Write. Therefore, the Governments should take it upon themselves to Distribute Copies of **"Belgiculture!"** Book 124, to all of their Soldiers and Sailors to Read, who can take it upon themselves to Send Copies to their own Families and Friends, and Encourage them to Read this Exceptionally Good Book, who can take it upon themselves to take Copies to their Friends and Naaberz: beCause, X-number of People are too Degenerated to read anything, much less, Understand it, who will Need some Help. And then, after Distributing these Books to those Soldiers, which will get them Inspired to Build those **"GLORIOUS Swanky Hotels Castles and Fortresses!"** (**Beautiful Planned City States for WISE Intelligent Well-Educated People with Common Sense and Good Understanding!**) **By The Worldwide People's Revolution!®** Book 019B, it will be Time to have those Soldiers March in the Streets, with their Bands Playing: ♫ *When the Saints go Marching in!* Yes, they can pass out Copies on the Streets, to whomever shows up to Watch them in the Parades. Moreover, each of 100 Soldiers can have a Special Book in his Hands, whereby they can Stand in Groups to be Photographed with the Books held up. †§‡

08-20 [_] O Selected King of "The New RIGHTEOUS One-World Government!" those Voluntary Soldiers could also be Furnished with some Hand-carved Leather Bags for Carrying the extra Copies of these Inspired Books, to Distribute on those Streets; but, only to whomever Promises to Read them: beCause many People will not Promise, while others will only Lie about it; but, God will Curse them for Lying, if you put a Curse on them for it, whereby they will Learn that it does not Pay to Lie, and Especially about anything so Serious as this. After all, we are Talking about the SALVATION of ALL of Mankind from the Darkness of Ignorance, which will be made Possible by: "The GREAT Worldwide TELEVISED Court HEARING!" (That Great Meeting of the Most-Intelligent and Well-Educated Minds!) By The Worldwide People's Revolution!® Book 041B, which **"Belgiculture"** will Inspire, which will eventually End ALL Wars, Worldwide! — that is, if we are DILIGENT to Do our DUTY, as Believers! †§‡

— Chapter 09 —

The DUTY of True Believers!

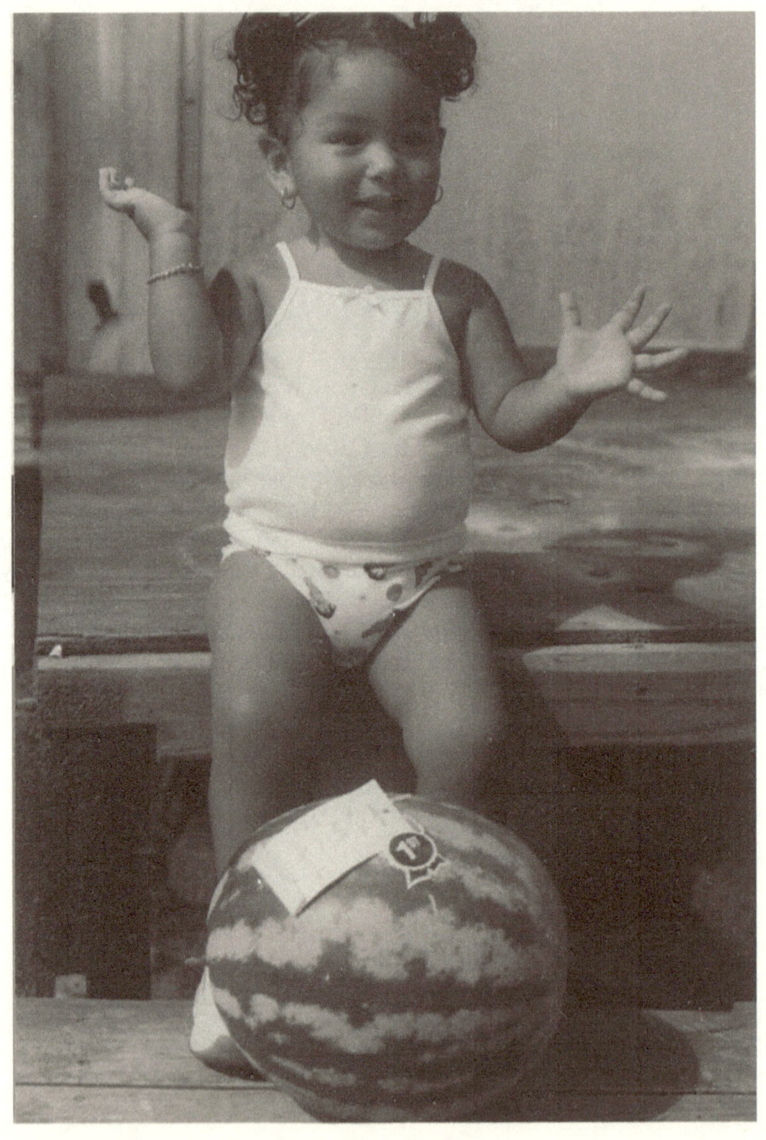

09-01 [_] O Selected King of "The New RIGHTEOUS One-World Government!" you have such a Wonderful Plan for the Salvation of Mankind! It is just AMAZING, to me! Imagine, "Seven Great Armies of Working Soldiers!" (HOW to Provide a Way for Everyone to WORK: so as to Eliminate Poverty, Crimes, Drug Abuses, Prisons and Unnecessary Taxes!) By The Worldwide People's Revolution!® Book 015B, being Furnished with all of the Necessary Tools and Equipment for Building those "GLORIOUS Swanky Hotels Castles and Fortresses!" (Beautiful Planned City States for WISE Intelligent Well-Educated People with Common Sense and Good Understanding!) By The Worldwide People's Revolution!® Book 019B, with an Unlimited Supply of New Money, which must be EARNED by Honest Labor, without Selling any Trash, nor Telling any Lies! Can you Imagine it? Honest WORKING Soldiers, who have Well-Trained Officers in Charge of them, who have Attended Special Classes in Unique Schools, who are Architects, Engineers, Soil Scientists, Horticulturists, and All-Mineral Organic Gardeners, who can Teach those Working Soldiers how to Grow their own Foods, and make their own Uniforms, and Parade through the Streets of Sin City with Good Gifts for the Poor Ignorant Tax Slaves, who never Tasted of a Really GOOD Watermelon, for Example, who never got to Eat at one of those "Royal Swanky Buffets!" (The Best Feasts in the Whole World!) By The Worldwide People's Revolution!® Book 103, which might have 50,000 Different Kinds of Fruits, Nuts, Vegetables, Flowers, and Delicious Dishes of Wholesome Natural Foods to Eat! †§‡

09-02 |_| Well, my Sweet Friend, all of those Good Things are Possible, and much, MUCH more, just by Trashing the False Ownership Doctrine of the Devil, whereby those Lying Conniving Edomites have made the Masses of Poor People into Education Slaves, Work Slaves, Tax Slaves, Insurance Slaves, Interest Slaves, Rent Slaves, Transportation Slaves,

Repair Bills Slaves, Home-owner Bills Slaves, Mortgage Bills Slaves, Entertainment Bills Slaves, and all of those other Kinds of SLAVES that were only Mentioned in Verse 08-10, which did not give the Countless Details in a thousand Books: beCause, each Family has a Book full of Details about their Bills, and all of their Struggles to come up with the Unnecessary Money for Paying their Bills, and often just enough Money to Barely Survive from Paycheck to Paycheck, who will soon be Wondering how they could be "Modern Deceived SLAVES!" (10 Simple Steps for Liberating ALL Modern Slaves, Worldwide, Including Yourself!) **By Liberty and Justice for ALL!** Book 113, for so Long, and not Realize that no Mountain Goats ever got themselves into such FAT Pickle Barrels.

09-03 [_] O Selected King, how is that Extremely Poor Man to be SAVED? He has Ears, even as most People do; but, he cannot Hear "HOW to Make America (and all other Nations) Really GREAT Without Telling any LIES!" (The Founding Fathers would have Loved it!) By The Worldwide People's Revolution!® Book 092. Indeed, he cannot even Hear "What is The GREATEST SIN?" (And it is NOT Blasphemy Against the Holy Spirit!) By The Worldwide

People's Revolution!® Book 091: beCause, he Suffers with Chronic Constipation of his Mind! ‡

09-04 [_] Well, my Friend, Believe it or not, there is a Way that such a Person can be Saved, which is Carefully Explained in: **"The Proper RULES for FASTING!" (The Complete Instruction Manual for True Repentance!) By The Worldwide People's Revolution!®** Book 046, which no such Person would Want to Study: beCause it is Em-bare-assing, as the Irreverent LOUDMOUTH Sloth-gut Windbag Hole-in-Thy-Head might say, who never Mentions Dietary Sins in his Lifeless Sermons: beCause he does not Want to Offend any FAT HOGS, nor Walruses with Bad Breaths, who might put some Change in his Offering Plate, who say that this Literature is not Politically Correct: beCause, those People are SICK and DISEASED, which they cannot Help to Cure: beCause, they have never Studied, **"Did God or Satan Ordain Medical Doctors?" (Ask Huck Finn and/or Nigger Jim: because neither Tom Sawyer nor Judge Thatcher would Know!) By The Worldwide People's Revolution!®** Book 022B. However, it is his DUTY to Teach Truths, no matter WHO is Offended, which he can Do with Love and Kindness, without going into the Details about their Stinking Farts, Odious Bathrooms, Putrid Vomit, and Unbearable Operations, when the Dr. Niif must Cut them Open, and Remove Tumors as BIG as Basketballs! Yes, it is GRUESOME, and should be Shown to ALL of the School Children, who might Think Twice about Eating another Pizza, Hamburger, Iced-cream, Pie, Cake, Cookie, Candy, Coke, or whatever it is that is making them so FAT and DISGUSTING, whereby they cannot even Run and Play with those Wild Mountain Goats, who might Look Stupid; but, at least they have no Bills to Pay, and can Leap UP by 20 feet from a Standing Point: beCause they are very STRONG! †§‡§§

09-05 [_] O Selected King of "**The New RIGHTEOUS One-World Government!**" it used to be during the Time of Moses, that Ministers or Priests were Paid to Teach the Truth, and everyone was Forced to Listen to their Sermons, while Standing on their Feet: so that they would not go to Sleep. Therefore, we should Return to those Good Old Days, and Console those Ministers with our Tithes and Offerings, whereby they would be Free to Speak Provable TRUTHS, INCLUDING ANY TRUTHS THAT MIGHT OFFEND A WICKED GOVERNMENT. Indeed, that is what the Story of Elijah was / is all about, who had to Remove the Heads of the Baal Worshipers with his own Sword, who were the POSSESSION Worshipers, who Believed in that False Ownership Doctrine of the Devil, which must be put into the Trash Can, along with those Trainloads of Pills and Doctor Bills: beCause, none of those Evil Things are Needed for True Prosperity. But, if you Doubt it, just Ask those Wild Mountain Goats, who have no Pills nor any Doctor Bills, who can Leap right Over the Heads of those Medical Snakes, whose Symbol on their Doorways shows 2 Snakes Kissing each other, while Wrapped around a Sword, which Symbolizes ROBBERY! †§‡§§

09-06 [_] Well, my Friend, there is only one Reason WHY that Young Man is Smoking that Stinking Cigarette: beCause, he is ADDICTED to it, and HATES it; but, he does not know HOW to Overcome it: beCause, he has never Heard of those "Beautiful Swanky FASTING SANITARIUMS!" (HOW to Learn Good Self-Discipline!) **By The Worldwide People's Revolution!®** Book 115. Indeed, you cannot Find such a Fasting Sanitarium in the entire World!

09-07 [_] O Selected King, what is to be Done for the Millions of Addicted Liars, who are Unwilling to Confess that they are Addicted to a Weed, who are SLAVES of Bad Habits? †§‡§§

09-08 [_] Well, my Friend, they should be Committed to those "Swanky Institutions for Compassionate Corrections!" (How to Correct even the Most-Stubborn Bullies!) **By The Biggest Bully of All Bullies!** Book 116, who will be Thanking us for Saving their Lives! †§‡§§

09-09 [_] O Selected King, those Capitalist Hogs have Managed to Pollute the entire World with their Weeds, and all Kinds of Ungodly Poisons. Therefore, how will we be Able to Correct them, and especially if they say that your New Government is Depriving them of their Freedom? †§‡§§

09-10 |_| Well, my Friend, all such Problems will be Solved, just by Conducting: "The GREAT Worldwide TELEVISED Court HEARING!" (That Great Meeting of the Most-Intelligent and Well-Educated Minds!) By The Worldwide People's Revolution!® Book 041B, which will put those Medical Snakes to Open Shame: beCause, they Know for a Fact that DRUGS are Inventions of Satan and Sons, Incorporated! Indeed, what Verse in the entire *Holy Bible* Recommends that anyone should Consume Drugs? You cannot Find any such Verse: beCause, it does not Exist. But, there is a Verse that clearly states that, *"... all of the Nations are Deceived by the Abundance of Babylon's Drugs."* — *NMV of Revelation 18:23.* Therefore, that is something to Think about. Yes, the Merchants of the Earth have been made Rich by the Abundance of her Drugs. *"Sorceries"* is *Drugs* in Greek, which comes from *Pharmaceuticals.* Moreover, the Fake Translators did not Want the Masses of People to Learn that bit of Important Information: beCause some of them were in the Business of Selling Drugs; or, they had Friends who were in that Business. Nevertheless, it Survived in *Strong's Exhaustive Concordance,* for whomever might be Seeking the Whole Truth, which we can Prove in the Courtroom, even if all Lying Snakes are Offended by it, whose Heads can be put on the Chopping Block, if they do not Confess the Whole Truth. For Example, I can Honestly say that I do not have a Pain in my entire Body, and I have not Consumed any of their Drugs for more than 50 Years; and very few People have done as much Difficult Work as I have done. Moreover, I have yet to Meet the Person who is Faster than I am. ‡

09-11 [_] O Selected King of "The New RIGHTEOUS One-World Government!" there are some of the 164 Concrete Blocks that you made with those Rough Rocks that can be seen in the Background, just to Build that 100,000-gallon Cistern. The Lower Half cannot be Seen, which is under the Sand, which is still under the Sand: beCause the Buyer never got enough Ambition to Clean it Out. Therefore, it only holds about 40,000 Gallons of Water, right now; but, it could be Cleaned Out, and might even Save some Lives, if it were Finished and Filled with Fresh Water. ‡

09-12 [_] Well, my Friend, there is a Part of the Balcony, which is 6 feet Wide, which we Filled with Rocks and Concrete during just one Day, on Top of 40 large Dump Truckloads of Sand, most of which I Shoveled and Wheeled into the Hole by myself, using a Wooden Ramp. It Worked Perfectly. The Cistern does not Leak, and it is Built on a Foundation of MUD. This next Picture shows what it looked like the next Morning, when I was the only Person there who got Out of Bed:

09-13 [_] As I Explained in several other Books, that Balcony makes it Possible to Clean the Upper Walls, without Climbing Down and Up and Down and Up a Tall Dangerous Ladder with both Hands Full, 40 Times, with a Cleaning Brush. The Cistern is 21 feet Deep, not counting the Cap on Top, which you can see after Verse 08-02, which made it Possible to Contain 100,000 Gallons of Water. Therefore, do not allow any Self-Deceived Beaver to tell you otherwise. It is possible to build a Concrete or Brick Dome on Top of the Concrete Cap; but, why be bothered with it, since we will soon be Building **"A New Jerusalem in the Great State of Flexible Texas!" (HOW to make Good Use of the Mississippi River!) By The Worldwide People's Revolution!® B-090?**

09-14 |_| ♦♦♦ O Selected King of **"The New RIGHTEOUS One-World Government!"** I am surprised that you still have faith in Mankind, after being Slandered, Robbed, Cheated, Poisoned, Mocked, and Mistreated for 70 Years, whose False Accusers will be most Ashamed of themselves during the Day of Judgment, when God says: "This Man did the Best he could with what he had to Work with, and with very little Money. Therefore, why do you Envy him? Why do you Speak Evil of him? Have you done any Better? Where is your Cistern for Water Storage? Are you not Aware that just after AIR, Water is the single most Important Thing for Survival?" Therefore, **"What will you Do when the Rain STOPS?" (God's Last Resort to Save Mankind from his MADNESS!) By The Worldwide People's Revolution!® Book** 101? Why do you Mock the **"101 Good Reasons and Great**

Advantages for Establishing a Righteous One-World Government!" **(Government By the People, Of the People, and For the People!) By The Worldwide People's Revolution!®** Book 104? Why do you not Study it, and Discover even more Great Advantages? As a Minister of Provable Truths, it is your God-given DUTY to Praise ALL that is GOOD, and to HATE ALL that is EVIL. Therefore, have you Done that, O Hypocrites? §‡

— Chapter 10 —

My Mindless Naaberz

10-01 [_] The Problem with Living in the City, or Out of it, is the Fact that your Mindless Naaberz can Spray all Kinds of Poisons into the Air, and there is nothing that you can Do about it: beCause, it is Legal, which is even Worse in Poor Countries, which have Weaker laws and regulations. †§‡

10-02 [_] There are a few of the 100 or so Stinking Capitalist Chicken Houses, which make it Possible for Poor People to Eat lots of Fried Chickens, which have been Fed GMO (Genetically-Modified Organisms) for their "Good Health," who have no Idea what a Wonderful Life it is! In Fact, if it got any more Wonderful, we might all Die from it. And some People say that Bill Computer Software Gates is Responsible for the Deaths and Diseases of thousands of People in Africa, whom he Assisted to get their Poisonous Shots. I would not Know for Sure; but, here is a Link to it

From a friend

U.K. apparently going to be the First Nation to be vaccinated with new CoOvid19 vaccine! Boris in talks with Mr & Mrs Gates. If you don't like what you read then don't worry, the government will ensure you don't have to make a choice.

MEET THE "REAL" BILL GATES.. IT'S NOT A PRETTY STORY.

There was a time Bill Gates vaccinated millions of women claiming it safe (HPV Vaccine) and sterilized them without their knowledge! Let's take a deep dive into Bill Gates' megalomaniacal vaccination program that he has planned for everyone, now that the people who stand to get very rich from a COoVID-19 vaccine are telling us that they want to force everyone to get the shot.

The nation of India, which struggles with sanitation and disease outbreaks, finally kicked Bill Gates out of the country in 2017. Why did that happen?

Back in 2000, the Bill and Melinda Gates Foundation offered a ton of money to India, in exchange for having its own handpicked "experts" put in charge of India's National Technical Advisory Group on Immunization (NTAGI).

Bill Gates' experts recommended that children in India be given FIFTY polio shots before age 5. The result between 2000 and 2017 was that 490,000 children in India were crippled with non-polio acute flaccid paralysis. It may not sound so bad to some , but non-polio acute flaccid paralysis is actually a horrible disease that leaves children paralyzed!!!

In another example in India, Gates funded an HPV vaccine that was administered to 23,000 girls in rural parts of the country (away from prying eyes, journalists and ethicists). According to a case that is now before the India Supreme Court, the Gates "doctors" bullied girls and their families into taking the shots, forged consent forms and then refused medical care to girls who were harmed by the vaccine. 5% of the girls immediately developed autoimmune and/or fertility disorders, and seven of the girls died after taking the shot.

Former CIA and Pentagon Advisor: "Millions of Americans are in DANGER!"

***We know a similar vaccine was given to our granddaughter this yr and two wks later she experienced her first seizure. Since has been diagnosed "New Onset Epilepsy"

You've probably heard about the Ted Talk that Bill Gates gave in 2010, in which he declared that vaccines "could reduce population." He gave the World Health Organization $10 billion around the same time that he made that declaration. Four years later, the nation of Kenya found out what those chilling words meant.

The WHO went into Kenya in 2014 and declared that every woman needed a tetanus shot due to a public health emergency. Not the men. It was only the women who were in danger of, you know... stepping on a rusty nail and developing tetanus. The goal was to get as many women as possible injected with the new "Bill Gates tetanus vaccine". When people were skeptical about this, the Kenyan government stepped in by helping the WHO administer forced vaccinations.

When millions of women who were forced to take the shot later realized that they could no longer get pregnant, the Catholic Doctors Association sent the Bill Gates tetanus vaccine out to independent labs for testing. Every single sample that was looked at by separate laboratories found a sterility formula in the tetanus shots.

The WHO denied it initially, but finally admitted that it had been working on a sterility vaccine since 2004. This isn't some Alex Jones conspiracy rant. These are facts that you can look up for yourself, which the garbage media in America conveniently declines to report on.

In 2002, the Gates Foundation funded an experimental meningitis vaccine in Africa, administered to 500 children. 10% of the kids were paralyzed by the vaccine.

Gates funded an experimental malaria vaccine trial in Africa in 2010, which was administered to about 6,000 babies. The result: 151 dead from the vaccine, and 20% of them suffered paralysis, seizures or febrile convulsions.

That's an awesome track record from a guy who wants to rush an untested koronaviirus vaccine into the marketplace while forcing everyone to get the shot. He wants to jab everyone (except himself & his own children) with a needle.

10-03 [_] I thot that the Share Button would have a Link for us to Click on; but, it did not. So, I just Copied it and Pasted it into this Book for everyone to Reed. I had to change the spelling on a few words: because Amazonico will not allow me to Publish any of those words: beCause, only the "Experts" are allowed to speak concerning such things. All that I am Asking for is: "The GREAT Worldwide TELEVISED Court HEARING!" (That Great Meeting of the Most-Intelligent and Well-Educated Minds!) By The Worldwide People's Revolution!® Book

041B, whereby we Tax Slaves might Learn the Whole Truth about it, even if we have to bring Bill and his Friends to Court with Shackles and Chains on, to Testify: beCause, Evil Things like that are very Upsetting to me; and I would like to Learn the Truth about it. How about yourself? †§‡§§

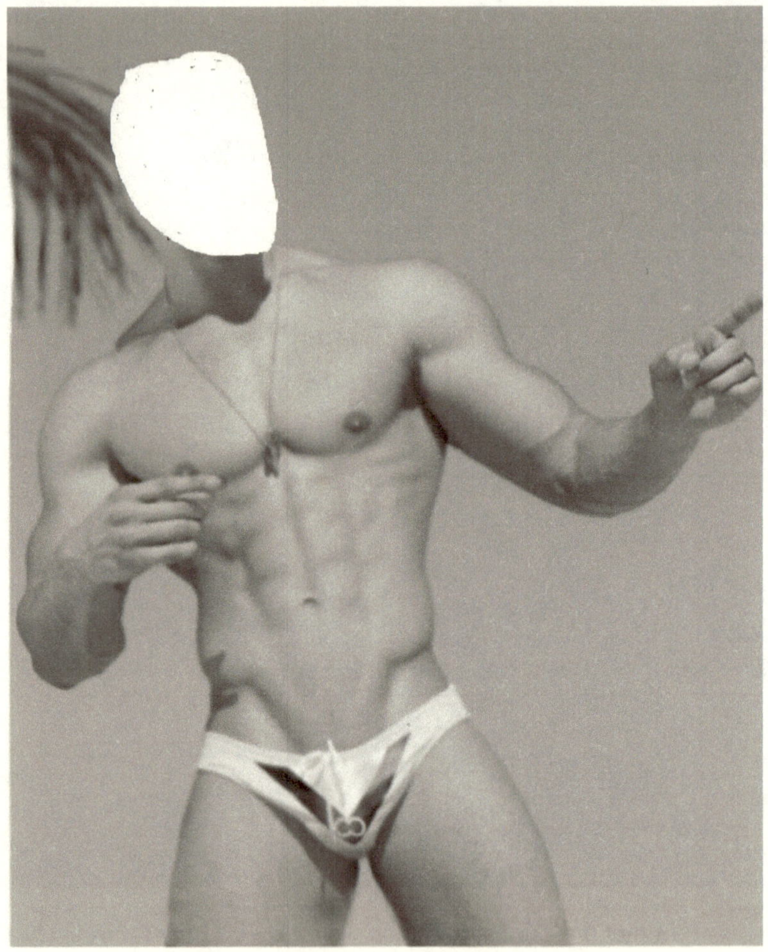

10-04 |_| O Selected King of "The New RIGHTEOUS One-World Government!" why would a Healthy Young Man like him Need any Shots of Pus? Does that make any Sense, at all? How about these Wild African Antelopes, do they also Need some EXPENSIVE Shots of PUS? †§‡§§

10-05 [_] Well, my Friend, according to Scientists, Wild Animals like those have Lived for Millions of Years in Africa, and without getting any Shots of Pus for anything. Therefore, there is a Good Chance that they will Liv for more Millions of Years, if People just leave them alone: beCause, it seems that People are a Curse to the Good Earth. Just Think, I have Heard that the Treatment for the Bug Costs thousands of Dollars per Person, and here is a Screen Shot of it for u:

- The average cost to treat a hospitalized patient with coronavirus is $30,000, according to a study.

- Regardless of the amount, the tab wouldn't be picked up entirely by patients with insurance.

- Even if you don't have coverage, you may not end up getting billed for all your treatment due to the Trump administration's intention to partially reimburse providers for treating the uninsured.

10-06 [_] So, O Selected King of **"The New RIGHTEOUS One-World Government!"** what would it Cost at a Swanky Fortress to Treat it? Surely, all such Rich People could Afford it? †§‡§§

10-07 [_] Well, it would hardly Cost anything, if we just Followed the Good Advice of Moses, Elijah, King David, Jeremiah, Isaiah, and King Jesus, which is Revealed in: **"Did God or Satan Ordain Medical Doctors?"** (Ask Huck Finn and/or Nigger Jim: because neither Tom

Sawyer nor Judge Thatcher would Know!) By The Worldwide People's Revolution!® Book 022B. †‡

10-08 [_] The one on the left was grown by "The LUSCIOUS All-Mineral Organic Method of Gardening!" (HOW to Grow DELICIOUS Satisfying Foods for Potential Kingz and Kweenz in Beautiful Swanky PALACES!) By The Worldwide People's

Revolution!® Book 021B, while the one on the right was grown by the Normal Chemical Method. Both Plants are the same Age. The one on the right was Strong, Tough, HOT, Bitter, and not fit to Eat; while the one on the left was Tender, Mild, Sweet, and very Pleasant to Eat. What more Evidence do we Need to Prove which Method of Gardening is Superior? Therefore, WHY would anyone Buy into the Modern Farming Method with Chemical Poisons of Various Kinds, when we could all be Eating GOOD Wholesome Natural Foods from our own Gardens? Am I the Crazy one; or, are Medical Snakes? †§‡

10-09 [_] Those Soldiers were "DRAFTED" into the Military, and Sent to Afghanistan to "Fight for America," they said. Why not Draft them to Grow Good All-Mineral Organic Vegetable Gardens, Fruit Trees, Nut Trees, Fragrant Flowers, and whatever we Need for True Prosperity? Why not Draft them to Help Build those "GLORIOUS Swanky Hotels Castles and Fortresses!" (Beautiful Planned City States for WISE Intelligent Well-Educated People with Common Sense and Good Understanding!) By The Worldwide People's Revolution!® Book 019B, and Pay them Double the Wages for doing it? Would they not be a lot Happier with that Plan, who could even bring their Wives with them, and Avoid Fornication in some Foreign Country? †§‡§§

10-10 [_] ♦♦♦ O Selected King of "The New RIGHTEOUS One-World Government!" those Murderous Soldiers seem to be fairly Happy to Fight for DUMBmocracy, which has no Voice of Common

Sense in **"The BIG White OUTHOUSE on the Not-so-Biblical Capitol DUNGHILL!" (The Chief Sins of the Divided States of United Lies!) By The Worldwide People's Revolution!® Book 023B.** In Fact, you have never Heard so much as one CONgressperson Speak about **"101 Good Reasons and Great Advantages for Establishing a Righteous One-World Government!" (Government By the People, Of the People, and For the People!) By The Worldwide People's Revolution!® Book 104:** beCause they are all Crazy.

10-11 [_] Well, my Friend, I would not go so far as to say that they are ALL Crazy; but, for Sure, at least some of them are Crazy, and most of them are Extremely IGNORANT, and cannot even Calculate their Numbers very well. For Example, they have Wasted TRILLIONS of Dollars on Military Games, and Lost Millions of Lives, and have nothing GOOD to Show for any of it! †§‡§§

10-12 [_] O Selected King of **"The New RIGHTEOUS One-World Government!"** what Great Effect would a Hydrogen Bomb have on that Small Stone Pyramid, which is only about 60 feet Tall? Suppose the Walls were at 45 Degree Angles, and 200 feet Tall, made of Solid Granite — would any Bomb have any Great Affects against it? Answer: NO, little or no Effect at all, and especially if that Wall were 100 feet THICK at the Base of it. However, I Like the Mighty Fortress that God Livz in, which is 1,500 Miles Tall, called the NEW JERUSALEM, in **"The New MAGNIFIED Version of the Book of REVELATION!" (The Understandable Version of the Most-Controversial Book in the Whole World!) By The Worldwide People's Revolution!® Book 105,**

whose Foundation Stones are 200 Miles THICK, which makes them Bomb-resistant.‡

10-13 [_] Well, my Friend, during World War 2, Heinrich Himmler built a Hardened Concrete House in Berlin, which was Attacked by the Russian Soldiers, who Lost 250 or so Men, in a Vain Effort to get Himmler, who, of course, was long Gone; but, he left 6 German Soldiers to Guard his House, who ran Out of Ammunition 3 Days later, and thus, Surrendered to the Russians. So, who Won that War? Himmler's House Won it, which is Proof that a House can be made Bomb-proof. However, Himmler's House was not nearly as Tough as a Swanky FORTRESS that is 100 Miles in Diameter, in 60 Great Stone TERRACES, with Stone Walls 100 Feet Tall and 50 feet Thick at the Base, with 200-Million "Beautiful Swanky Stone Dome Home COMPLEXES!" (HOW to Build SECURE Tax-proof, Insurance-proof, Self-air-conditioned, Paint-proof, Rot-proof, Termite-proof, Mouse-proof, Fireproof, Tornado-proof, Hurricane-proof, Thief-proof, and BOMB-PROOF Houses!) By The Worldwide People's Revolution!® Book 102, which would not easily be Conquered by any Bugs, Drones, Spies, nor Lies, and Especially if those People were Wise enough to Elect a RIGHTEOUS KING, to Enforce the Laws and Rules that they VOTE FOR.

10-14 [_] Please Notice that the Mountain in the Background is hardly Visible: beCause of the Air Pollution from those Stinking Dangerous Vehicles. Moreover, the Picture does not Show the 90-plus thousand Children with Asthma and other Lung Diseases from Breathing such Capitalist Air, much less, the 200,000 Victims of SLAVERY and their Boxes of BILLS to Pay, which would not Exist within "The Environmentalists' Perfect Paradise!" (HOW almost Everyone can be Living in a Beautiful Manmade Paradise!) By The Worldwide People's Revolution!® Book 035C: beCause of having "The Right Design for Living!" (A List of Great Advantages for Building Beautiful Planned City States!) By The Worldwide People's Revolution!® Book 012B. Indeed, "All of the Arguments are in Favor of our Selected King, who has Zero Challengers!" (Before you Attend another Election Deception, you should Carefully Study this Inspired Book with an Honest Open Mind!) By The Worldwide People's Revolution!® Book 085, which is a Companion Book of: "Are Americans the Most-STUPID People who ever Lived?" (HOW Working People can PROSPER and Live in PEACE Under the Rulership of a RIGHTEOUS KING!) By The Worldwide People's Revolution!® Book 047. Therefore, Study it, and especially if you are a Government Official: beCause, you could put your Name on the Historical Map as a Defender of the CHRISTIAN FAITH, who Loves ALL that is GOOD! †‡

— Chapter 11 —

The Next Step on the Highway of Life!

11-01 [_] Many People Think that this Inspired Book should be much Longer, and have at least 40 Chapters, just to Deal with some of the Major Problems that are not Covered within this Book — such as Gay Marriages, which is Thoroughly Addressed in: "How GAY is GOD?" (Oh, the Wonders of it all, when it ALL Hangs Out!) By The Worldwide People's Revolution!® Book 071, which goes into Great Details to Explain the Gayness of some of the Gods, including Jehovah God, who Forbids Sodomy; but, not Gay Marriages, like that of Jonathan and David, nor that of Jesus and John, who were True Lovers, which is Explained in Great Details in: "The Gospel According to our Elected King!" (The Good News from the Most Modern Perspective!) By The Worldwide People's Revolution!® Book 077, which no one has Proven to be WRong. †§‡

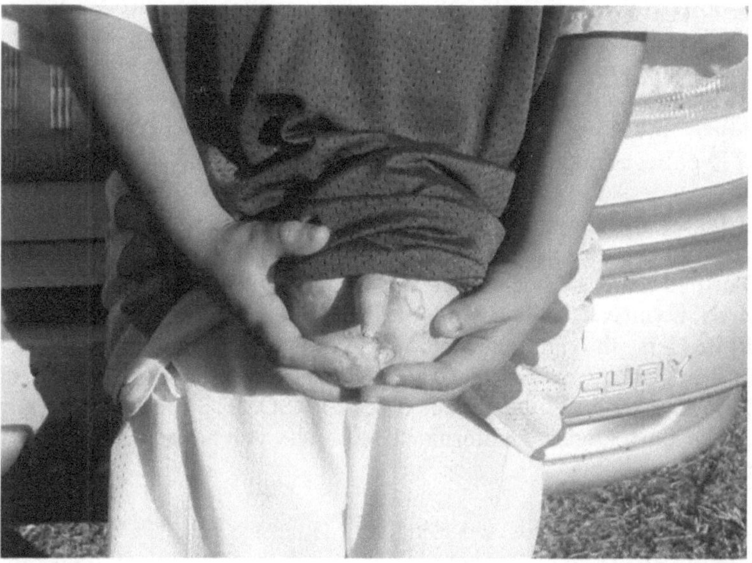

11-02 [_] For Example, WHY would God put a Penis on a Sweet Potato, if he were not at least Partly GAY? Some Carrots are Obviously having Frot Sex; but, most are Straight, and Proud of it.

11-03 [_] O Selected King of "The New RIGHTEOUS One-World Government!" do you Plan on getting Married in: "The Great World TEMPLE of PEACE!" (The Glory of Jerusalem Arises Again in the Great State of Flexible Texas!) By The Worldwide People's Revolution!® Book 017B? Will that be "The END of CONFUSION!" (The Great CELEBRATION of the Magnificent Wedding of the Most-Humble, Honest Nations, and the Grand Year of JUBILEE!) By The Worldwide People's Revolution!® Book 050? If so, I can hardly Wait for the CLIMAX! Will everyone be Dancing Naked in the Streets with King David? *2 Samuel 6:16.*‡

11-04 [_] Well, my Friend, I do Plan on getting Married in "The Great World TEMPLE of PEACE!" which will be a MASS WEDDING of about 7 Million People, if we can Discover them.

11-05 [_] So, O Elected King of "The New RIGHTEOUS One-World Government!" will that be a GAY Marriage, or what, since you have never been Married? Will it be a Grand ORGY? †§‡

11-06 [_] Of course NOT! Why would you Want an ORGY? We are Civilized People, I Hope. §‡

11-07 [_] Well, O Elected King of "The New RIGHTEOUS One-World Government!" it will not Hurt anything to have a little Fun, will it? Even Jesus might Appear, to have some New Wine!

11-08 [_] Well, my Friend, if he does Appear in all of his Naked Glory, we will have the Grandest Wedding in World History: beCause, in his Glorified State, he is about 400 Feet TALL! Yes, he is a GIANT of a MAN, if you can Believe it, or not. The Problem will be getting his Great White Horse through the Doorway, since he is also more than 400 Feet Tall! In Fact, he must be that Tall, just to be Seen as a little Speck in the Dark Awesome Rolling Clouds of a FEARSOME Sky from New York City to Lost Angels, Californicate — unless you have a Better Plan to make him Visible.

11-09 [_] Well, O Elected King of "The New RIGHTEOUS One-World Government!" we could just Watch them on TV, and Save him from all of that Trouble to Giantize himself and his Great White Horse, which must be quite an Elaborate Process, I would Think, if not Impossible!

11-10 [_] Well, until he Appears, we will never Know for Sure just what is going on in Heaven. ‡

— Chapter 12 —

The Conclusion!

12-01 [_] O Selected King of "The New RIGHTEOUS One-World Government!" we Readers will never Know for Sure if you are Serious, or just another Joker in the Deck of Capitalist Cards.

12-02 [_] Well, my Friend, no matter how it turns out, I am the Winner in this Race to the Little White Outhouse, which is Explained in: "The CONDENSED Version of MARK TWAIN Races for the PRESIDENCY with a Landslide VICTORY!" (The 2020 Presidential Candidates Desperately Need Some STRONG Undefeatable COMPETITION!) By The Worldwide People's Revolution!® Book 033C. Therefore, you will just have to take the Time to STUDY it!

12-03 [_] O Elected King of "The New RIGHTEOUS One-World Government!" I can hardly Wait to See you Mounted on your Golden Throne, in "The Great World TEMPLE of PEACE!" (The Glory of Jerusalem Arises Again in the Great State of Flexible Texas!) By The Worldwide People's Revolution!® Book 017B, which will Truly be a Great Year of JUBILEE!!

12-04 [_] ♦♦♦ Well, my Friend, just Imagine how Wonderful it would be, if everyone in the Whole World Cheerfully went along with my Master Plan for Worldwide Law, Order, Obedience, Peace and True Prosperity, without any Silly Arguments, nor even any Untimely Trials at: "The GREAT Worldwide TELEVISED Court HEARING!" (That Great Meeting of the Most-Intelligent and Well-Educated Minds!) By The Worldwide People's Revolution!® Book 041B: beCause it is Possible to, "VOTE for The GOAT!" (The New Political Party that has Guaranteed Solutions for our Massive Problems!) By The Worldwide People's Revolution!® Book 109!§

12-05 [_] Well, O Elected King of "The New RIGHTEOUS One-World Government!" I would say that it would be a LANDSLIDE VICTORY, just as you have Written it; but, HOW could it Happen, seeing that almost no one has Heard of you? Would they Believe anything in this Book?

12-06 [_] Well, my Friend, if they do not Check the Appropriate Boxes with Statements that they Agree with, and 100%, I would say that this World has gone to Hell, and Satan is in Charge of it!

12-07 [_] Well, O Elected King of "The New RIGHTEOUS One-World Government!" I would say that you are 100% Riit about that — except that we have not yet Tried the Experiment, and Mailed Exact Copies of this Inspired Book to the Leaders of all Nations, who might be too Ashamed to show their Faces, at: "The GREAT Worldwide TELEVISED Court HEARING!" (That Great Meeting of the Most-Intelligent and Well-Educated Minds!) By The Worldwide People's Revolution!® Book 041B, which could Prove to be very Em-BARE-assing, for them! ‡

12-08 [_] So, my Friend, the next Step is to make Sure that every Leader of every Nation gets a Copy of this Inspired Book in their own Language, if that is Possible, including President Donald Trump and his Cabinet of Political Puppets, who Speak a very Strange Unknown Language, who most likely never Heard about those "GLORIOUS Swanky Hotels Castles and Fortresses!" (Beautiful Planned City States for WISE Intelligent Well-Educated People with Common Sense and Good Understanding!) By The Worldwide People's Revolution!® Book 019B: beCause of never taking the Time to Study, "C-SPAN-DEX!" (Your Filtered View of Bad Government!) By The Worldwide People's Revolution!® Book 097, which is a Companion Book of: "The New MAGNIFIED Version of the HOLY KORAN!" (WHY MuhamMAD went to Hell for Spiritual MURDER!) By The Worldwide People's Revolution!® Book 089.†

12-09 [_] O Elected King of "The New RIGHTEOUS One-World Government!" I would say that it is Impossible to Communicate with Spiritually Dead People, who have Ears that cannot Hear. However, with President Trump, it is not a Case of Deafness, nor of Blindness of the Mind; but, only of a Lack of MONEY, which will be his Silly Childish Argument Against the Swanky Fortress System, which you have Solved by the Establishment of "The New RIGHTEOUS One-World Government!" which he will also Vote for: beCause he is no doubt Sick and Tired of this Capitalist Nonsense. After all, he is 74 Years Old, which is Plenty of Time for a Person to Learn what is Good for everyone, which is for every Family to get Set Up Properly for Living and Working at Home, in their own Private Gardens of Eden, which is an Inherited Thing within our Souls, which we are all Born with, who Know Instinctively that Adam and Eve were Set Up Properly by Jehovah God, himself, who is BISEXUAL, even though he never did get Married; but, he Adopted a Chosen Son, called Jesus Christ, and got the Holy Ghost to Implant a Chosen Seed in the Womb of Mary, while Joseph and Mary were Sleeping: beCause, that Ghost had to get into Joseph's Sperm Bank, and Discover that Chosen Seed, which was Passed Down all of the Way from Adam, through Abraham, Isaac, Jacob, and Joseph — just as it is Written in: "The New MAGNIFIED Version of The GOOD NEWS According to Saint LUKE!" (The Magnified Gospel of Saint Luke in Plain English!) By The Worldwide People's Revolution!® Book 061, which is one of the Best Books on this Good Earth, which is a Companion Book of: "The New MAGNIFIED Version of the Book of ACTS!" (The Understandable Version of the Acts of the Apostles in Plain English!) By The Worldwide People's Revolution!® Book 063, which Explains HOW and WHY the First Church had *"… all Material Things in Common among them."*

12-10 [_] Well, my Friend, I See that I have Finished another Beautiful and Inspired Book, which everyone in the Whole World should get to Reed with an Honest Open Mind, and before the Election Deception Day: beCause they might Want to, "VOTE for The GOAT!" (The New Political Party that has Guaranteed Solutions for our Massive Problems!) By The Worldwide People's Revolution!® Book 109. Yes, they only need to Write it on a Piece of Paper, and Mail it to the Speaker of the House of Representatives in Washington, District of Chief Criminals, who will not know what to Do with 200-Million similar Letters from 200-Million Different Addresses!

12-11 [_] O Elected King of "The New RIGHTEOUS One-World Government!" I would say that if you do not have any Challengers, that makes you the Elected King by DEFAULT! [_] Amen

12-12 [_] Well, my Friend, that is also Exactly HOW that I Feel about it; but, if anyone Disagrees, they should Check the above Box with a Red-X Mark, and get Prepared for "The GREAT Worldwide TELEVISED Court HEARING!" (That Great Meeting of the Most-Intelligent and Well-Educated Minds!) By The Worldwide People's Revolution!® Book 041B: beCause, one Way or another, we are going to WIN this Race with a Landslide VICTORY! So Help us God!

— Chapter 13 —

The Appendix — a List of Definitions

13-01 [_] This Appendix contains Common Expressions of Speech in English Nonsense. Enjoy!

Why do we say scot free?

The expression **'Scot-free'** originates from the Scandanavian word, 'Skat,' which means "tax" or "payment." The word mutated into **'scot'** as the name of redistributive taxation meant to provide relief to the poor during the 10th century.

www.gingersoftware.com › content › phrases › scot-free
'Scot-Free' | Phrase Definition, Origin, & Examples - Ginger Software

Is it an insult to people from Scotland? A: Contrary to what you may think, **"scot free"** has nothing to do with Scotland or the Scots. ... Nowadays, according to The American Heritage Dictionary of the English Language, to get off **"scot free"** can mean either to avoid paying for something or to escape punishment. Mar 21, 2007

www.grammarphobia.com › blog › 2007/03 › is-scot-free...
Is "scot free" a slur on Scots? - The Grammarphobia Blog

Getting away with something **"scot free"** has nothing to do with the Scots (or **Scotch**). The **scot** was a medieval tax; if you evaded paying it you got off **scot free**. Some people wrongly suppose this phrase alludes to Dred **Scott**, the American slave who unsuccessfully sued for his freedom. May 30, 2016

brians.wsu.edu › 2016/05/30 › scotch-free-scot-free
scotch free / scot free | Common Errors in English Usage and More ...

13-02 [_] Where does the Expression, "Son of a Gun" come from?

The **phrase** potentially has its origin in a Royal Navy direction that pregnant women aboard smaller naval vessels give birth in the space between the broadside **guns**, in order to keep the gangways and crew decks clear.

en.wikipedia.org › wiki › Son_of_a_gun
Son of a gun - Wikipedia

Originally Answered: Is **"son of a gun"** a **bad word**? Not exactly. The most commonly repeated version of the etymology of the phrase is that the British Navy used to allow women to live on naval ships. Any child born on board who had uncertain paternity would be listed in the ship's log as **"son of a gun."**

www.quora.com › Is-son-of-a-gun-a-bad-word
Is 'son of a gun' a bad word? - Quora

English Language Learners **Definition** of **son of a gun**

US, informal. : a person (especially a man) or thing that **you** are annoyed with. old-fashioned —used by a man to address a male friend. —used to express mild surprise, disappointment, etc.

www.merriam-webster.com › dictionary
Son Of A Gun | Definition of Son Of A Gun by Merriam-Webster

13-03 [_] Where did "Bite the Bullet" come from?

It is often stated that it is derived historically from the practice of having a patient clench a **bullet** in his or her teeth as a way to cope with the extreme pain of a surgical procedure without anesthetic, though evidence for **biting** a **bullet** rather than a leather strap during surgery is sparse.

en.wikipedia.org › wiki › Bite_the_bullet
Bite the bullet - Wikipedia

To **"bite** the **bullet"** is to endure a painful or otherwise unpleasant situation that is seen as unavoidable. The phrase was first recorded by Rudyard Kipling in his 1891 novel The Light that Failed.

13-04 [_] What does it Mean to "Call a Spade a Spade"?

It is also referred to as "let's **call a spade a spade**, not a gardening tool" which refers to **calling** something "as it is", that is, by its right or proper name, without "beating about the bush"—being outspoken about it, truthfully, frankly, and directly, even to the point of being blunt or rude, and even if the subject ...

en.wikipedia.org › wiki › Call_a_spade_a_spade
Call a spade a spade - Wikipedia

"To **call a spade a spade**" entered the English language when Nicholas Udall translated Erasmus in 1542. Famous authors who have used it in their works include Charles Dickens and W. Somerset Maugham, among others. Sep 23, 2013

www.npr.org › sections › codeswitch › 2013/09/19 › is-it...
Is It Racist To 'Call A Spade A Spade'? : Code Switch : NPR

13-05 [_] What does the Phrase, "Great Scott" Mean?

"Great Scott!" is an interjection of surprise, amazement, or dismay. It is a distinctive but inoffensive exclamation, popular in the second half of the 19th century and the early 20th century, and now considered dated.

en.wikipedia.org › wiki › Great_Scott
Great Scott - Wikipedia

Origins. It is frequently assumed that **Great Scott**! is a minced oath of some sort, **Scott** replacing God. The 2010 edition of the Oxford Dictionary of English labels the **expression** as "dated" and simply identifies it as an "arbitrary euphemism for **Great** God!".

13-06 [_] What does "Fighting Tooth and Nail" Mean?

fight tooth and nail. Engage in vigorous combat or make a strenuous effort, using all one's resources. For example, I'm going to **fight tooth and nail** for that promotion. This expression, with its allusion to biting and scratching, was first recorded in 1576.

www.dictionary.com › browse › fight-tooth-and-nail
Fight tooth and nail | Definition of Fight tooth and nail at Dictionary.com

13-07 [_] Why do People say, "For Pete's Sake!"?

"For **Pete's sake**" originated as a substitute for "for Christ's **sake**," and other similar expressions. According to the Oxford English Dictionary, "for **Pete's sake**" came into use more than a century ago and prompted similar sayings such as "for the love of **Pete**" in 1906 and "in the name of **Pete**" in 1942. Feb 21, 2013

www.usatoday.com › story › opinion › 2013/02/21 › neu...
Neuharth: 'For Pete's sake!' How did it start? - USA Today

13-08 [_] What does it Mean — "Has the Cat got your Tongue?"

Definition of **cat got your tongue**

—used to ask someone why he or she is not saying anything"You've been unusually quiet tonight," she said.

www.merriam-webster.com › dictionary
Cat Got Your Tongue - Merriam-Webster

13-09 [_] "Fornicate you," or "Breed you," was shortened to F*** you.

Eliot poem called "The Triumph of Bullshit." The origin of "fuck" is one of the hardest to trace, as it was banned from early written work and dictionaries. Etymologies from various sources all tend to agree that the **word** probably developed from various Germanic languages. The verb form of the **word** in German is ficken. Mar 25, 2017

mashable.com › 2017/03/25 › origin-of-swear-words
The surprising origins of your f*cking favorite swear words - Mashable

13-10 [_] What does "to have a Chip on your Shoulder" Mean?

To have a **chip** on one's **shoulder** refers to the act of holding a grudge or grievance that readily provokes disputation. It can also **mean** a person thinking too much of oneself (often without the credentials) or feeling entitled.

en.wikipedia.org › wiki › Chip_on_shoulder
Chip on shoulder - Wikipedia

13-11 [_] Can you "Catch a Bullet"?

Yes. The "**bullet catch**" is a common magic trick in which a magician appears to **catch** a fired **bullet** in mid-flight—often between their teeth. This an illusion, of course; it's not possible to **catch a bullet** like that. ... A **bullet** fired straight up would eventually reach a maximum height.

what-if.xkcd.com › ...
Catch! - What If? - xkcd

13-12 [_] What is the Slang Meaning for "Spade"?

Slang: Extremely Disparaging and Offensive. a contemptuous term used to refer to a black person.

www.dictionary.com › browse › spade
Spade | Definition of Spade at Dictionary.com

In gardening, a **spade** is a hand tool **used to** dig or loosen ground, or to break up lumps in the soil. Together with the fork it forms one of the chief implements wielded by the hand in agriculture and horticulture. It is sometimes considered a type of shovel.

en.wikipedia.org › wiki › Spade
Spade - Wikipedia

13-13 [_] What does it Mean to be "Long in the Tooth"?

long in the tooth. Getting on in years, old, as in Aunt Aggie's a **little long in the tooth** to be helping us move. This expression alludes to a horse's gums receding with age and making the **teeth** appear **longer**. [

www.dictionary.com › browse › long--in--the--tooth
Long in the tooth | Definition of Long in the tooth at Dictionary.com

13-14 [_] What does it Mean to "Knuckle Under"?

knuckle under. Also, **knuckle** down. Give in, acknowledge defeat, as in The dean refused to **knuckle under** to the graduate students' demands, or He was forced to **knuckle** down before their threats of violence. Presumably this idiom alludes to a kneeling position with hands on the ground, knuckles down. [

www.dictionary.com › browse › knuckle--under
Knuckle under | Definition of Knuckle under at Dictionary.com

13-15 [_] What does it Mean, "for the Sake of" something, or someone?

Also for one's **sake**. Out of consideration or regard for a person or thing; for someone's or something's advantage or good. For example, For Jill's **sake** we **did** not serve meat, or We have to stop fighting for the **sake** of family unity. [

www.dictionary.com › browse › for-the-sake-of
For the sake of | Definition of For the sake of at Dictionary.com

13-16 [_] What does, "Cut to the Chase" Mean?

"Cut to the chase" is a **phrase** that **means** to get to the point without wasting time. The **saying** originated from early film studios' silent films. It was a favorite of, and thought to have been coined by, Hal Roach Sr.

en.wikipedia.org › wiki › Cut_to_the_chase
Cut to the chase - Wikipedia

13-17 [_] What does "going Cold Turkey" Mean?

The phrase "taking **cold turkey**" has also been reported during the 1920s as slang for pleading guilty. The term **is** also attributed to piloerection or "goose bumps" that occurs with abrupt withdrawal from opioids, which resembles the skin of a plucked refrigerated **turkey**.

en.wikipedia.org › wiki › Cold_turkey
Cold turkey - Wikipedia

13-18 [_] Where did "it's no Skin Off my Back" come from?

Surprisingly, this phrase hasn't been around for too long. First used in the early twentieth century, **its** variations include "**no skin off my** nose" and "**no skin off my** teeth." Of course, "**no skin off my back**" is the most common version in America, and it comes from the age-old punishment of flogging. Aug 7, 2014

www.ericksonliving.com › tribune › articles › 2014/08
Where'd that phrase come from? (Aug 7, 2014) | Erickson Living

13-19 [_] Where did, "It's a Wash" come from?

—used to say that something is equal and that one side does not have an advantageYou won the first game and I won the second, so it's a **wash**.

www.merriam-webster.com › dictionary
It's A Wash | Definition of It's A Wash by Merriam-Webster

13-20 [_] Where does "Holy Smoke" come from, if not from Censers in the Hands of Priests? Not even Merriam nor Webster knew about Holy Smoke, or Burning Incense. See *Leviticus 10.*

Definition of **holy smoke**. informal. —used to say that one is very surprised, pleased, or excited**Holy smoke!**

www.merriam-webster.com › dictionary
Holy Smoke | Definition of Holy Smoke by Merriam-Webster

13-21 [_] What is the "B Word"? The *Holy Bible* uses both Bastard and Bitch. A Bastard is a Person who was Born of Fornication, without a Holy WedLOCK. A Bitch is a Female Dog, or a Person who Acts like a Female Dog that is in Heat, who Desperately Needs some Sexual Relief, before Committing some Crime, like Rape, which is often followed by Murder: beCause the Rapist does not Want to take a Chance on being Exposed as a Rapist. Therefore, he Murders the Victim of his Aggression, which Happens about 3,000 Times, on Average, in Houston, Texas, each Year, whereby the Victims are usually Young Teenage Boys and Girls, who are Prostituting themselves for Money, which is one of the Bitterest Fruits of Capitalism, which is Eliminated by Swanky Fortresses: beCause any Teenager, even at 12 Years of Age, can get lots of Work with Good Pay.

From Wikipedia, the free encyclopedia. The "b" **word** is a euphemism generally used to replace a profane **word** starting with the letter **b**. The profanity in question may be: Bastard. Bitch.

en.wikipedia.org › wiki › B_word
B word - Wikipedia

13-22 [_] What does "P" stand for at the End of an Epistle, or Letter?

A postscript (**P.S.**) is an afterthought, thought that's occurring after the letter has been written and signed. The term comes from the Latin post scriptum, an expression **meaning** "written after" (which may be interpreted in the sense of "that which comes after the writing").

en.wikipedia.org › wiki › Postscript
Postscript - Wikipedia

13-23 [_] What does it Mean, "Do not Throw the Baby Out with the Bath Water"? Some Critical People discover something WRong within an otherwise Good Book — including the *Holy Bible* — and therefore they Throw Out the Whole Book, or put it into the Trash Can of their own Minds.

"**Don't throw the baby out with the bathwater**" is an idiomatic **expression** for an avoidable error in which something good is eliminated when trying to get rid of something bad, or in other words, rejecting the favorable along with the unfavorable.

en.wikipedia.org › wiki › Don't_throw_the_baby_out_wit
Don't throw the baby out with the bathwater - Wikipedia

13-24 [_] What does it Mean, that "Blood is Thicker than Water"? It is Referring to a Relationship.

Blood is thicker than water is a medieval proverb in English that **means** that familial bonds will always be stronger **than** bonds of friendship or love.

en.wikipedia.org › wiki › Blood_is_thicker_than_water
Blood is thicker than water - Wikipedia

13-25 [_] What does it Mean to, "Beat around the Bush"? — a Long Delay in getting to the Point. Medical Doctors usually Beat around the Bush when someone is about to Die: beCause, they do not Want to Offend, nor Frighten anyone with the Raw Unvarnished Truth of it. Death comes to everyone, sooner or later; but, it is possible to Postpone it, even for Years, by Fasting and Praying.

beat around/about the **bush**, to avoid coming to the point; delay in approaching a subject directly: Stop **beating around the bush** and tell me what you want. **beat** the bushes, to scout or search for persons or things far and wide: **beating** the bushes for engineers.

www.dictionary.com › browse › beat--around--the--bush
Beat around the bush | Definition of Beat around ... - Dictionary.com

{FOOTNOTE: Never Fast without Following "The Proper RULES for FASTING!" (The Complete Instruction Manual for True

Repentance!) By The Worldwide People's Revolution!® Book 046: beCause, you might Kill your Ignorant self; and I am NOT Beating around the Bush about it; but, I am Telling it just like it is. Do all Things with True Nolij, as King Solomon Warned, and do not Presume that you Know anything about anything, just beCause you have Heard this or that. For Example, I heard that a Woman Died from not Eating for only 3 Days, which was just a Lie: beCause, she Died from Chronic Constipation, from not Eating enough Juicy Fruits, which might Run Through her Bowels more Fluently than Constipating Meats, Cheeses, Peanut Butter, Sticky Gooey PASTE-treez, Iced-creams, Spaghetti, Noodles, Gummy Dumplings and other Constipating Foods, which they would find Difficult to Run Through a Clean Pipe.} †§‡

13-26 [_] What does it Mean to "Give someone the Third Degree"? For Example, George Warmonger Bush and Little Dick Chicanery should be Ordered to COURT, and Threatened with being Boiled to Death in HOT Used Motor Oil, if they do not Confess to the False Flag Operations of September 11th, 2001; or else, Explain just HOW that Hardened Steel Column sliced itself Off at a 45° Angle, without Beating around the Bush: beCause, even a 6-year-old Child Knows for a Fact that it was NOT Done by any Airplanes. However, if someone Sincerely Believes that it was Done by an Airplane, they should get Together with Like-minded Fools, and Prove it in COURT!

The **third degree** is a euphemism for torture ("Inflicting of pain, physical or mental, to extract confessions or statements").

en.wikipedia.org › wiki › Third_degree_(interrogation)
Third degree (interrogation) - Wikipedia

13-27 [_] Where did Common Sayings come from?

Many everyday **phrases** are nautical in origin— "taken aback," "loose cannon" and "high and dry" all **originated** at sea—but perhaps the most surprising example is the **common** saying "by and large." As far back as the 16th century, the word "large" was used to mean that a ship was sailing with the wind at its back. Apr 23, 2013

www.history.com › news › 10-common-sayings-with-hist...
10 Common Sayings With Historical Origins - HISTORY

13-28 [_] What does "Sell like Hotcakes" Mean? A Book like this one should Sell like Hotdogs.

sell/go **like hot cakes**, to be disposed of very quickly and effortlessly, especially in quantity: His record sold **like hot cakes** on the first day after its release.

www.dictionary.com › browse › sell--like--hot--cakes
Sell like hot cakes | Definition of Sell like hot cakes at Dictionary.com

13-29 [__] What is the "C" Word? In the Future, it will be Referring to COURT, as in going to Court to be Tried for TREASON, for Betraying the Holy Church of Provable Truths. For Example, Little Dick Chicanery will not Like to Confess that he Gained 58 Billion Dollars by going to War in Iraq, much less, that Rich Edomite Bankers gained about 3 Trillion Dollars from it! Therefore, it will be the Trial of the Century, or C Hearing, which will Prove to be very Em-BARE-assing! ‡

Cunt (/kʌnt/) is a vulgar **word** for the vulva or vagina and is also used as a term of disparagement. ... The earliest known use of the **word**, according to the Oxford English Dictionary, was as part of a placename of a London street, Gropecunt Lane, **c.**

en.wikipedia.org › wiki › Cunt
Cunt - Wikipedia

13-30 [__] What was the First Swear Word?
Fart, as it turns out, is one of the oldest rude **words** we have in the language: Its **first** record pops up in roughly 1250, meaning that if you were to travel 800 years back in time just to let one rip, everyone would at least be able to agree upon what that should be called. Dec 23, 2014

www.fastcompany.com › the-oldest-english-swear-words-...
The Oldest English Swear Words, Visualized - Fast Company

13-31 [__] Can you Legally Swear at the Police in the United Kingdom (UK)?
There is no specific offence of **swearing** at a **police** officer, and in fact it is not a specific crime of **swearing** in public, only of causing "harassment alarm or distress" under the Act mentioned above. This requires some evidence of an individual being, or being likely to be, offended by the language used. Nov 21, 2011

www.fosters-solicitors.co.uk › news › crime › is-it-ok-to-s...
Is It OK To Swear At The Police? - Fosters Solicitors

13-32 [__] What does it Mean, that "they are a Dime a Dozen"?

dime a dozen. So plentiful as to be valueless. For example, Don't bother to buy one of these—they're a **dime a dozen**. The **dime** was declared the American ten-cent coin in 1786 by the Continental Congress. [

www.dictionary.com › browse › dime--a--dozen
Dime a dozen | Definition of Dime a dozen at Dictionary.com

13-33 [_] What does it Mean to be "Caught with your Pants Down"? In the Case of former President George Walking Bush and Little Dick Chicanery, their Pants are always down around their Ankles: beCause several Nations have Outstanding Arrest Warrants for them as War Criminals of the Worst Kind, who just Naturally FEAR **"The GWTCH!"** (See Book 041B.)

Be surprised in an embarrassing or guilty posture, as in We spent a lot of time preparing for the inspection; we didn't want to get **caught** with our **pants down**. This phrase presumably alludes to someone's **pants** being lowered to attend to bathroom needs but is not considered particularly vulgar.

www.dictionary.com › browse › caught-with-one-s-pants-...
Caught with one's pants down, be | Definition of Caught with one's ...

13-34 [_] What does it Mean, "It is like Pulling Teeth"? Well, in the Case of getting "The GREAT Worldwide TELEVISED Court HEARING!" (That Great Meeting of the Most-Intelligent and Well-Educated Minds!) By The Worldwide People's Revolution!® Book 041B, under way, it is like Pulling Teeth: beCause, all of the Outlaws are Dead Set Against it. Therefore, it will be the Truest Test of the Righteousness of Americans, who must Demand it, if they are Righteous, just to have Good Consciences during the Day of Judgment, when God Asks: "What is your Explanation for just HOW that Hardened Steel Column got Cut Off? Could you not See that it was NOT the Dirty Work of Osama bin Laden, O Fool?" And you will say, "O Lordy, I iz Extreemlee IgnuRUNT, having almost no Braanz at all!" And God will say, "Therefore, why should I let you into my Holy Kingdom with Intelligent, Wel-Ejukaatid People?" And you will have to Confess that you are Unworthy, O SINator Blabbermouth, Chirping Brainless Bird, the Third or Fourth. §§

Definition of like **pulling teeth**

—used to say that something is very difficult and frustratingGetting him to make a decision is like **pulling teeth**.

www.merriam-webster.com › dictionary
Like Pulling Teeth | Definition of Like Pulling ... - Merriam-Webster

13-35 [_] What is the Fastest Bullet in the World?

The . 220 Swift remains the **fastest** commercial cartridge in the **world**, with a published velocity of 4,665 ft/s (1,422 m/s) using a 29 grain **bullet** and 42 grains of 3031 powder.

en.wikipedia.org › wiki › .220_Swift
.220 Swift - Wikipedia

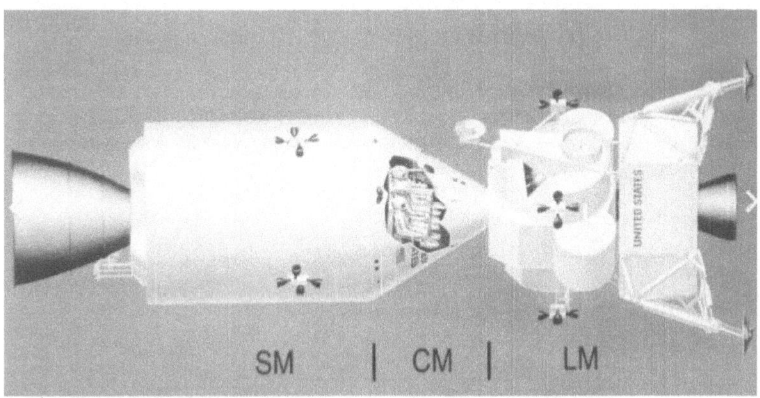

13-36 [_] The LEM (Lunar Escape Module), which is shown just above LM in the Screen Shot, supposedly Departed from the Moon at 4,000 Miles per Hour (MpH), back in July of 1969, with Neil Armstrong and Buzz Aldrin inside of it, somewhere, after crawling through the Nose of the Service Module (SM), while leaving the Part with "United States" written on it, behind, on the Moon, after spending 21 Hours and 36 Minutes on it. The Amazing thing about it, was how it Departed from the Moon with only 8 Gallons of Rocketdyne Fuel, when it Required nearly a Million Gallons of Rocketdyne Fuel to get it up there! It also had to have had enough Fuel to run the Air-conditioning Equipment for some Time, in Temperatures as Hot as the Oven in a Stove. The AstroNOT's Backpacks contained Water-cooled Air-conditioners, according to NASA. Whatever the Case, it all Needs to be Proven at "The GREAT Worldwide TELEVISED Court HEARING!": beCause there are more than 10,000 Websites that Dispute the Moon-landing HOAX. And there might be 10,000 Engineers that Agree with **"EXPERTS SPEAK OUT!"** †§‡

13-37 [_] What does it Mean … ?

"**Cutting off** the **nose to spite** the **face**" is an expression to describe a needlessly self-destructive over-reaction to a problem: "Don't **cut off your nose to spite your face**" is a warning against acting out of pique, or against pursuing revenge in a way **that would** damage oneself more than the object of one's anger.

en.wikipedia.org › wiki › Cutting_off_the_nose_to_spite_...
Cutting off the nose to spite the face - Wikipedia

13-38 [_] Who said "Still Waters Run Deep"?

A **quiet** person may be very profound, as in Susie rarely **says** much, but **still waters run deep**. The physical observation in this term dates from ancient times, but it has been used figuratively since about 1400. Anthony Trollope amplified it in He Knew He Was Right (1869): "That's what I call **still water**.

www.dictionary.com › browse › still-waters-run-deep
Still waters run deep - Dictionary.com

13-39 [_] Where does "Break a Leg" come from?

Superstition against wishing an actor Good Luck! has led to the adoption of this phrase in its place. Popular etymology derives the phrase from the 1865 assassination of Abraham Lincoln. John Wilkes Booth, the actor turned assassin, leapt to the stage of Ford's Theater after the murder, **breaking** his **leg** in the process.

www.theatrecrafts.com › glossary-of-technical-theatre-terms
More about Break A Leg – Theatrecrafts.com

13-40 [_] What does "Beating a Dead Horse" Mean?

Flogging a **dead horse** (alternatively **beating a dead horse**; or **beating a dead** dog in some parts of the Anglophone world) is an idiom that **means** a particular effort is a waste of time as there will be no outcome, such as in the example of flogging a **dead horse**, which will not cause it to feel pain or anything else.

en.wikipedia.org › wiki › Flogging_a_dead_horse
Flogging a dead horse - Wikipedia

13-41 [_] Why is a Third-degree Burn less Severe than a First-degree Murder?

The **higher** the **gauge** number, the smaller the diameter and the thinner the **wire**. Since thicker **wire** carries more current because it has less electrical resistance over a given length, thicker **wire** is **better** for longer distances.

searchnetworking.techtarget.com › definition › American-...
What is American Wire Gauge (AWG)? - Definition from WhatIs.com

What happens if wire gauge is too big?

There may be mechanical drawbacks. The heavier **gauge wire** will be stiffer, making it more difficult to work with and, **if** considerably heavier than needed, may be larger than the terminals on the devices can take. Aug 30, 2009

sawmillcreek.org › showthread › 119340-Wire-gauge-too...
Wire gauge too big? - Sawmill Creek Woodworking

GAUGE	SWG DIAMETER (Inches)	AWG DIAMETER (Millimeters)
14 Gauge Wire	0.0800 in	1.626 mm
16 Gauge Wire	0.0640 in	1.290 mm
18 Gauge Wire	0.0480 in	1.024 mm
20 Gauge Wire	0.0360 in	0.8128 mm

13-42 [_] Does anything in America make Good Sense?

American exceptionalism is one of three related ideas: The first is that the history of the United States is inherently different from that of other nations. ... This ideology itself is often referred to as "**American exceptionalism**." Second is the idea that the US has a unique mission to transform the world.

en.wikipedia.org › wiki › American_exceptionalism
American exceptionalism - Wikipedia

Among them was the **idea** that all people are created equal, whether European, Native **American**, or African **American**, and that these people have fundamental rights, such as liberty, free speech, freedom of religion, due process of law, and freedom of assembly. **America's** revolutionaries openly discussed these concepts.

www.loc.gov › exhibits › founded-on-a-set-of-beliefs
Founded on a Set of Beliefs - Creating the United States ...

Early **examples** of the term's usage do include a declaration made at the 1930 **American** Communist convention proclaiming "the storm of the economic crisis in the United States blew down the house of cards of **American exceptionalism**".

en.wikipedia.org › wiki › American_exceptionalism
American exceptionalism - Wikipedia

Historian Richard B. Morris in 1973 identified the following seven figures as key **Founding** Fathers: John Adams, Benjamin Franklin, Alexander Hamilton, John Jay, Thomas Jefferson, James Madison, and George Washington based on the critical and substantive roles they played in the formation of the country's new government ...

en.wikipedia.org › wiki › Founding_Fathers_of_the_Unit...
Founding Fathers of the United States - Wikipedia

Today's **American Dream** is being able to graduate from college with minimal debt, secure a job in your field that has benefits, be able to afford health care costs (while saving for retirement and paying down loans), and still live a comfortable life. Jun 25, 2019

www.investopedia.com › articles › investing › what-ameri...
What is the American Dream in 2016? - Investopedia

The actual phrase "**American exceptionalism**" was originally coined by Soviet leader Joseph Stalin in 1929 as a critique of a revisionist faction of **American** communists who argued that the **American** political climate was unique, making it an 'exception' to certain elements of Marxist theory.

en.wikipedia.org › wiki › American_exceptionalism
American exceptionalism - Wikipedia

The **US** economy is far bigger than that of any other rich, advanced nation. ... The sustained higher rate of real GDP growth in the **United States** over a longer period of time has resulted in a substantially higher level of real GDP per capita in the **United States** than in other major industrial countries. Mar 13, 2017

www.aei.org › economics › 10-reasons-why-america-is-so...
10 reasons why America is so much richer than other rich nations ...

13-43 [_] Who was the Father of America?

Father of Our Country. On April 30, 1789, in a deep, low voice, George Washington gave his first speech as president of the United States. This speech is now **known** as the first presidential inaugural address.

www.americaslibrary.gov › jb_nation_gwashington_1
Father of Our Country - America's Story from America's Library

13-44 [_] How did George Washington gain his Wealth?

Like most 18th and early 19th century Virginia planters, **Washington was** asset rich but cash poor. **His** assets were partially earned through work (surveying, officer salary), financial investments (personal bonds and some corporate equities) and the net proceeds of **his** plantation (Mt.

www.moaf.org › checks_balances › washington_family ▾
We're Wealthy Already and Bound to Get Richer | Museum of ...

In 1789, **his** salary **was** 2% of the U.S. budget and he owned over 50,000 acres of land. In addition to this, **George** held several positions before, during and after the presidency; he **was** also a surveyor, soldier, farmer and distiller. It is likely, however, that most of **his wealth** can be traced to **his** land speculations. Dec 27, 2017

www.wellsfm.com › blog › george-washingtons-finances
George Washington's Finances - Wells Financial Management

The **Washington** family was a **wealthy** Virginia family which had made its fortune in land speculation. ... **George Washington** was **born** February 22, 1732, at Popes Creek in Westmoreland County, Virginia, and was the first of six children of Augustine and Mary Ball **Washington**.

en.wikipedia.org › wiki › George_Washington
George Washington - Wikipedia

He had an estimated net **worth** of $525 million, in today's dollars. Feb 19, 2018

www.businessinsider.com › george-washington-richest-pr...

The life of George Washington, who was once the richest president ...

Debt and depreciation often meant that a **president's** net worth was less than $0 at the time of his death. Most **presidents** before 1845 were extremely **wealthy**, especially Andrew Jackson (who was born into poverty) and **George Washington**. ... Truman, all **presidents** since this time have been millionaires.

en.wikipedia.org › wiki › List_of_presidents_of_the_Unit...
List of presidents of the United States by net worth - Wikipedia

13-45 [_] Who is the Richest President in the World?

Who is the richest president in the World 2020?

By far, the **richest president in the world** is Russia's Vladimir Putin. May 28, 2020

www.foxbusiness.com › lifestyle › who-is-the-richest-pres...
Who is the richest president in the world? | Fox Business

The **richest president in history** is Donald Trump, who is the first billionaire **president**. His net worth, however, is not precisely known because the Trump Organization is privately held.

en.wikipedia.org › wiki › List_of_presidents_of_the_Unit...
List of presidents of the United States by net worth - Wikipedia

According to this survey compiled in 2010, George Washington would be worth half a billion in today's dollars. John Hancock may have been the **wealthiest Founder** who never became president. He inherited a successful import-export business called the House of Hancock from an uncle and increased its value.

www.quora.com › Who-was-the-wealthiest-Founding-Fat...
Who was the wealthiest Founding Father? - Quora

The world's **poorest man** Jerome Kerviel has handed himself in to French authorities. Jerome Kerviel, the ex-Societe Generale trader who has more debt than anyone else in the world, has turned himself in to French authorities to begin a three-year jail sentence. Sep 17, 2015

www.cityam.com › world-s-poorest-man-just-handed-him...
The world's poorest man Jerome Kerviel has handed himself in to ...

The world's **richest women** — and how they're supporting pandemic causes. Alice Walton of Walmart is worth a reported $54.4 billion, making her the world's **richest woman.** Apr 9, 2020

www.bizjournals.com › news › latest-news › 2020/04 › th...
The world's richest women — and how they're supporting pandemic ..

America's 18th **president**, Ulysses S. Grant, **died broke**. He lost $100,000 after being defrauded by his son's business partner, Ferdinand Ward, which forced him into bankruptcy. Even before that, though, Grant had a reputation for spending more money than he had. Oct 25, 2019

www.investopedia.com › the-5-poorest-u-s-presidents-47...
The 5 Poorest U.S. Presidents - Investopedia

Qatar is, by far, the **richest country in the world**, with a GNI per capita of $116,799 -- more than $20,000 higher than any other nation. The **country** has more in oil reserves than all but two other **countries** worldwide -- equal to 13% of the global supply. Jul 7, 2019

www.usatoday.com › story › money › 2019/07/07 › riche...
Qatar, China, Singapore: Top 25 richest countries in the world

All told, at least 12 chief executives—over a quarter of all American presidents—were **slave** owners during **their** lifetimes. Of these, eight held enslaved people while in office. **The** "peculiar institution" loomed large over **the** first few decades of American presidential history. Jul 19, 2017

www.history.com › news › how-many-u-s-presidents-own...
How Many U.S. Presidents Owned Slaves? - HISTORY

13-46 [_] Who has the most Brains?

The average score on an **IQ** test is 100. Most people fall within the 85 to 114 range. Any score over 140 is considered a high **IQ**. A score over 160 is considered a **genius IQ.** Oct 23, 2012

www.businessinsider.com › smartest-people-on-earth-201...
Smartest People On Earth - Business Insider

{FOOTNOTE: Not that it matters much; but, my Military IQ was 186, which gained me the Rank of Specialist E-4: beCause I never got to Work in the Field that I was Trained for, which was Hercules Missiles, which became Obsolete by the Time that I Graduated from School.}

13-47 [_] What was Jesus' Social Status?

We know in general he was low **class**, by the standards of the Roman imperial aristocracy or even of the ruling **class** of Palestine, the Herodian client kings. But he may have been an artisan. He doesn't seem to have been a peasant in the strict sense, someone who was working the land for a living.

www.pbs.org › wgbh › pages › frontline › shows › religion

Jesus Many Faces - Jesus' Social Class | From Jesus To Christ ...

Jesus looked at him and **said**, "How hard it is for the **rich** to enter the kingdom of heaven! Indeed, it is easier for a camel to go through the eye of a needle than for someone who is **rich** to enter the kingdom of heaven."

en.wikipedia.org › wiki › Jesus_and_the_rich_young_man

Jesus and the rich young man - Wikipedia

Wealth, according to the **Bible**, is like fire, good but dangerous. Everyone sees the good, so the **Bible** warns us about the danger. Danger one: the desire to get **rich** (I Timothy 6:10). Danger two: worry about money (Matthew 6:25-34). Jul 8, 2016

www.geneva.edu › blog › faith › can-a-christian-be-rich-...

Can you be rich and be a Christian? - Geneva College, a Christian ..

2 Corinthians 8:9 (NIV)

"For you know the grace of our Lord Jesus Christ, that though he was **rich**, yet for your sake he became **poor**, so that you through his **poverty** might **become rich**." Sep 4, 2019

www.worldvision.org › christian-faith-news-stories › what...

What does the Bible say about poverty? | World Vision

The Great Revolt began in the year 66 CE, during the twelfth year of the reign of Nero, originating in **Roman** and **Jewish** religious tensions. The crisis escalated due to anti-taxation protests and attacks upon **Roman** citizens by the **Jews**.

en.wikipedia.org › wiki

First Jewish–Roman War - Wikipedia

In the King James Version of the Bible the text reads: Not every one that saith unto me, Lord, Lord, **shall. enter** into the kingdom of **heaven**; but he that doeth. the **will** of my Father which is in **heaven**.

en.wikipedia.org › wiki › Matthew_7:21

Matthew 7:21 - Wikipedia

{FOOTNOTE: I do Hope to God that Teachers in the Kingdom, which is coming to the Earth from Heaven, have more Brains than the WikiNumbskulls have, who put Periods (.) where they do not Belong. For Example, why are there Periods after "shall" and "doeth"? Why not Quote my Version?, which reedz: "Not every Person who says unto me, 'O Lordy, I Bleevz in yu,' shall Enter into the Kingdom of God, which is coming to the Earth from Heaven; but, only he who Does the Will of my Heavenly Father, who Livz Inside of Jupiter, who is about 400 feet Tall, with a Beard that is about 50 feet Long, and a Tally Whacker to Match it, with 2 Chime Bells as big as 70-gallon Barrels! Indeed, that is why he is called the 'Lord of Glory,' you must Understand. But, that is not all: beCause his Brains are about 200,000,000 Times as Big as our own, just to be Able to Keep Track of everything that is going on within his Solar System." §§}

13-48 [_] Can a Nation be Rich and also Greatly in Debt?

"**Money** and possessions are the second most referenced topic in the **Bible – money** is mentioned more than 800 **times** – and the message is clear: Nowhere in **Scripture** is debt viewed in a positive way." May 24, 2012

www.forbes.com › sites › sherylnancenash › 2012/05/24
Is The Bible The Ultimate Financial Guide? - Forbes

What did Rich men ask Jesus?

First, **Jesus** advises the **man** to obey the commandments. When the **man** responds that he already observes them, and **asks** what else he can do, **Jesus** adds: If you want to be perfect, go, sell your possessions and give to the poor, and you will have treasure in heaven.

en.wikipedia.org › wiki › Jesus_and_the_rich_young_man
Jesus and the rich young man - Wikipedia

A popular current text, the King James Version shows 1 Timothy 6:10 to be: For the love of **money** is the **root of all** of **evil**: which while some coveted after, they have erred from the faith, and pierced themselves through with many sorrows.

en.wikipedia.org › wiki › Love_of_money
Love of money - Wikipedia

What country is deepest in debt?

List of countries by external debt

Rank	Country/Region	Per capita US dollars
1	United States	77,000
2	United Kingdom	127,000
3	Germany	65,600
4	Netherlands	265,400

Not one of its 1,200 mostly uninhabited coral islands measure more than six feet (1.8 meters) above sea level. The **Maldives** – made up of a chain of nearly 1,200 mostly uninhabited islands in the Indian Ocean – is the lowest country in the world. Feb 7, 2014

earthsky.org › earth › maldives-lowest-country-in-the-wo...
Maldives is the world's lowest country | Earth | EarthSky

{FOOTNOTE: Economically-speaking, the Divided States of United Debts is the Lowest Nation in the World, being about 180 feet Under the Water, you might say, with a Long Proverbial "Snorkel" for getting some Air from Beijing, China, which could get Cut Off at just any Time!}

Among the economies we study, Australia **has the highest household debt**-to-GDP ratio (Figure 1), followed by South Korea, Malaysia, and Thailand. China **has** witnessed the fastest **household debt** growth. Jun 27, 2019

www.theasianbanker.com › updates-and-articles › househ...
Household debt highest in Australia, while China sees fastest ...

The national **debt** (or government **debt**) of the People's Republic of **China** is the total amount of money owed by the government and all state organizations and government branches of **China**. As of May 2020, it stands at approximately CN¥ 39 trillion (US$ 5.48 trillion), equivalent to about 48.4% of GDP.

en.wikipedia.org › wiki › National_debt_of_China
National debt of China - Wikipedia

It's unlikely America **will** ever **pay off its** national **debt**. It doesn't need to while creditors remain confident they **will** be repaid. ... First, the **U.S.** economy has historically outpaced **its debt**. For example, the **U.S. debt** at the end of World War II was $260 billion.

www.thebalance.com › will-the-u-s-debt-ever-be-paid-off...
Will the U.S. Debt Ever Be Paid Off? - The Balance

Just about every **country** is in **debt**, but some are not so far in **debt** as western **countries**. The simple reason is these **countries** are not good risks, so lenders are not inclined to lend to them. Poor third world **countries** for instance, or Russia have fairly low **debt**.

www.quora.com › Are-there-any-countries-in-the-world-t...
Are there any countries in the world that are not in debt? - Quora

The public holds $19.7 trillion, or 77%, of the national debt. 1 Foreign governments hold about a third of the public debt, while the rest is owned by **U.S.** banks and investors; the Federal Reserve; mutual funds; state and local governments; and pensions funds, insurance companies, and savings bonds.

www.thebalance.com › who-owns-the-u-s-national-debt-3...
Who Owns the U.S. National Debt? How Much Is Owed?

13-49 [_] What Nation is most in Debt?

Japan, with its population of 127,185,332, has **the highest** national **debt** in the world at 234.18% of its GDP, followed by Greece at 181.78%. Japan's national **debt** currently sits at ¥1,028 trillion ($9.087 trillion USD).

worldpopulationreview.com › countries-by-national-debt
Debt to GDP Ratio by Country 2020 - World Population Review

The main cause of **Switzerland's** low indebtedness is a mechanism introduced by the Confederation to stabilise the federal **debt**: "the **debt** brake". Enabled in the Constitution since 2003, with a population approval rate of 85% in 2001, the rule has **strong** legitimacy and many cantons have introduced similar models. Mar 18, 2019

think.ing.com › articles › switzerland-why-not-enough-de...
Switzerland: Why too little debt could be a problem | Article | ING Think

{FOOTNOTE: It seems to be Suggesting that Debts are Good; but, are they? Do you Like to be in Debt, yourself? Most People are Greatly Bothered by it, if they Believe what the *Holy Bible* Teaches: *"Owe no man anything; but, to Love one another…" First Timothy 6.* I have always followed that Rule, when it was Possible. However, I did get Anxious, one Time, and ran up a Debt of about 400 Dollars, which I Paid Off in about 2 Months. I have no Plans for doing it again. However, the Federal Government says that each of us Owes about 77,000 Dollars. Sorry, but they will never get it out of my Bank Account: beCause, I keep it Empty: beCause I do not Trust Bankers, much less, the Federal Government Liars. I Remember the Great Depression.}

13-50 [_] How Deep in Debt are American Households?

The median **household** income hit $61,372 in 2017, according to the U.S. Census Bureau. That's almost $20,000 more than it was in 2000. But the **typical American household** now carries an **average debt** of $137,063.

www.debt.org › faqs › americans-in-debt › demographics
Consumer Debt Statistics & Demographics in America - Debt.org

{FOOTNOTE: I am Obviously NOT a Typical American. Moreover, I Suggest that ALL Debts should be Forgiven, Worldwide, and we Human Beings should Ring the Liberty Bell, and Declare a Worldwide Year of JUBILEE, according to *Leviticus 25.* After all, almost everyone will Appreciate it. And then, after that, we should Adopt "The New RIGHTEOUS One-World Government!" (HOW to Establish a Righteous One-World Government without Going to WAR!) By The Worldwide People's Revolution!® Book 056, and get to Work on the Construction of those "GLORIOUS Swanky Hotels Castles and Fortresses!" (Beautiful Planned City States for WISE

116

Intelligent Well-Educated People with Common Sense and Good Understanding!) By The Worldwide People's Revolution!® Book 019B, which will put an End to Poverty, forevermore: beCause, that is "The Right Design for Living!" (A List of Great Advantages for Building Beautiful Planned City States!) By The Worldwide People's Revolution!® Book 012B. See: "101 Good Reasons and Great Advantages for Establishing a Righteous One-World Government!" (Government By the People, Of the People, and For the People!) By The Worldwide People's Revolution!® Book 104, which is Linked to all of the Books in …}

— Chapter 40 —

A Long List of other Fascinating Literature by the same Inspired Author

[_] 40-001 — "LIGHTNING **Versus the** Lightning Bug!" (HOW almost Everyone can become Moderately RICH, without Telling Any Lies nor Selling Any Capitalist Trash!) By The Worldwide People's Revolution!® Book 001B.

[_] 40-002 — "What is WRong with those Professing Christians?" (A Self-Examination of the Heart of the Body of Good Government!) By The Worldwide People's Revolution!® Book 002B.

[_] 40-003 — "For the Love of Money!" (The Strange Things that People Say and Do to Get more Money!) By The Worldwide People's Revolution!® Book 003B.

[_] 40-004 — "How Best to Prepare for CLIMATE CHANGES!" (The Wisest Plan for Mankind to Follow!) By The Worldwide People's Revolution!® Book 004B.

[_] 40-005 — "Why do I have to be Surrounded by CRAZY PEOPLE!" (Do almost all People Feel like they are Surrounded by CRAZY People?) By The Worldwide People's Revolution!® Book 005B.

[_] 40-006 — "The Washington Journal is a FARCE! (C-SPAN Managers are not very WISE!) By The Worldwide People's Revolution!® Book 006C. (This Book has lots of Good Humor.)

[_] 40-007 — "The PRAYERS of PUMPKINHEADS!" (This Book is otherwise known as the Prayers of Preachers, Priests, Professors, Politicians, Prostitutes, Policemen, Pumpkinheads, Punks, Prisoners, and other Professionals — in other Words, the Capital P People!) By The Worldwide People's Revolution!® Book 007B. (Some of it is for Adults only.)

[_] 40-008 — "A Sound Argument for Good Masters and Obedient Servants!" (WHY Everyone Needs a Good Master, and every

Master Needs Good Obedient Servants!) By The Worldwide People's Revolution!® Book 008B.

[_] 40-009 — "WHY are some Preachers so POOR?" (HOW almost all Preachers can Get Moderately RICH, without Preaching any Outlandish LIES!) By The Worldwide People's Revolution!® Book 009B.

[_] 40-010 — "GOOD NEWS for REBEL WOMEN!" (HOW almost all Wives can become Moderately RICH without Leaving their Homes! Guaranteed!) By The Worldwide People's Revolution!® Book 010B.

[_] 40-011 — "The Low Court of Supreme Injustices is Brought to Trial!" (Our Selected King Butts Heads with the United States Supreme Court, with or without their Black Robes of Hypocrisies and Lies!) By The Worldwide People's Revolution!® Book 011B. (This Inspired Book contains the Famous *Declaration of Interdependence,* which is a Must Read. It also contains the Correct Wording for the Placard on the Statue of Liberty.)

[_] 40-012 — "The Right Design for Living!" (A List of Great Advantages for Building Beautiful Planned City States!) By The Worldwide People's Revolution!® Book 012B. (This Book contains many Important Drawings, as well as HOW to Save hundreds of Trillions of Dollars by Building Swanky Fortresses, and Living in Peace within them. It is a Companion Book of Book 011B, which contains many more Great Advantages for Swanky Fortresses.)

[_] 40-013 — **"The Gospel According to The Worldwide People's Revolution!®" (The Good News from the Most Modern Perspective!)** See Book 077. (This Book contains the Famous Sermon of Jonah to the Ninevites, whereby 120,000 People Repented in Sackcloth and Ashes! Do not Miss Out on it. Not even the Rev. Dr. Billy Graham got 120,000 Converts during one Day!)

[_] 40-014 — **"Poverty Hunger Riots Strikes Police Brutalities Election Deceptions and Civil Wars!" (The High Price that we Earthlings have Paid for Leaving the Good Land!) By The Worldwide People's Revolution!® Book 014B.**

[_] 40-015 — **"Seven Great Armies of Working Soldiers!" (HOW to Provide a Way for Everyone to WORK: so as to Eliminate Poverty,**

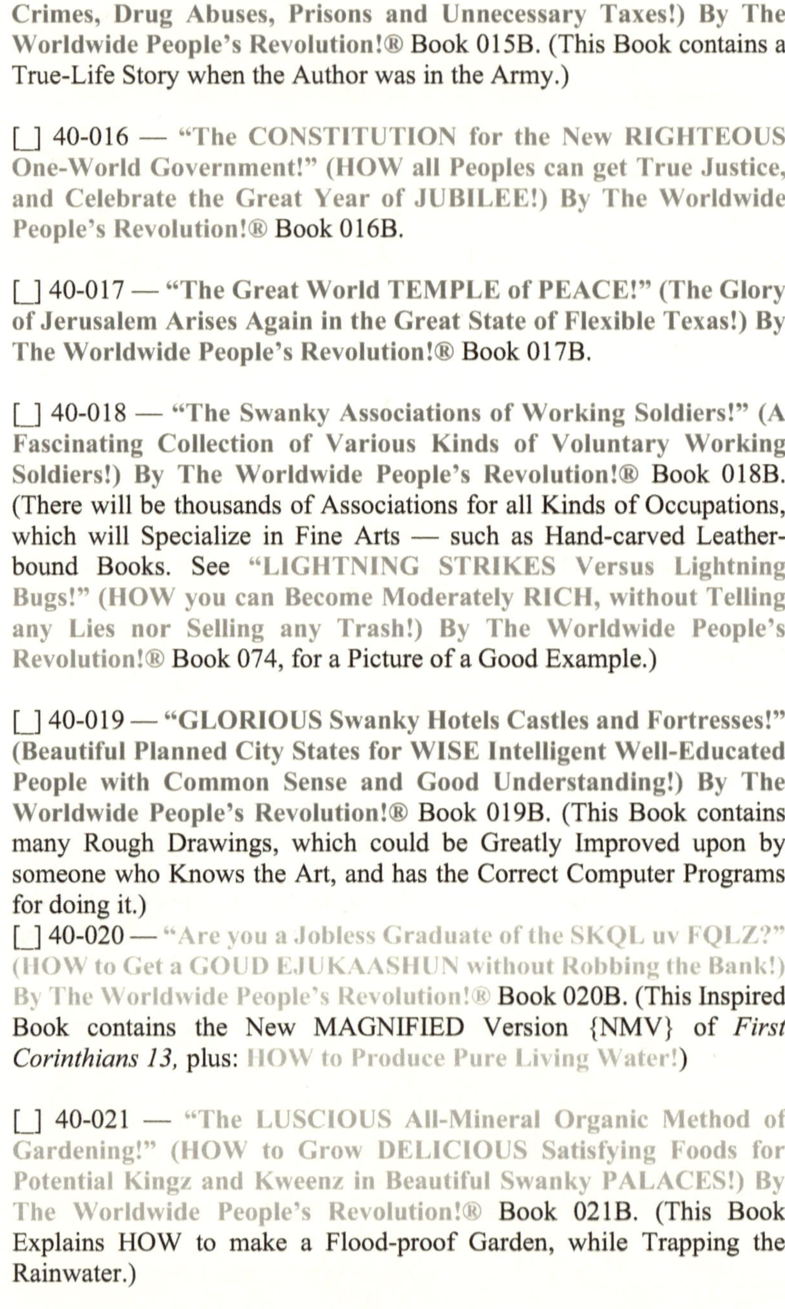

Crimes, Drug Abuses, Prisons and Unnecessary Taxes!) By The Worldwide People's Revolution!® Book 015B. (This Book contains a True-Life Story when the Author was in the Army.)

[_] 40-016 — "The CONSTITUTION for the New RIGHTEOUS One-World Government!" (HOW all Peoples can get True Justice, and Celebrate the Great Year of JUBILEE!) By The Worldwide People's Revolution!® Book 016B.

[_] 40-017 — "The Great World TEMPLE of PEACE!" (The Glory of Jerusalem Arises Again in the Great State of Flexible Texas!) By The Worldwide People's Revolution!® Book 017B.

[_] 40-018 — "The Swanky Associations of Working Soldiers!" (A Fascinating Collection of Various Kinds of Voluntary Working Soldiers!) By The Worldwide People's Revolution!® Book 018B. (There will be thousands of Associations for all Kinds of Occupations, which will Specialize in Fine Arts — such as Hand-carved Leather-bound Books. See "LIGHTNING STRIKES Versus Lightning Bugs!" (HOW you can Become Moderately RICH, without Telling any Lies nor Selling any Trash!) By The Worldwide People's Revolution!® Book 074, for a Picture of a Good Example.)

[_] 40-019 — "GLORIOUS Swanky Hotels Castles and Fortresses!" (Beautiful Planned City States for WISE Intelligent Well-Educated People with Common Sense and Good Understanding!) By The Worldwide People's Revolution!® Book 019B. (This Book contains many Rough Drawings, which could be Greatly Improved upon by someone who Knows the Art, and has the Correct Computer Programs for doing it.)
[_] 40-020 — "Are you a Jobless Graduate of the SKQL uv FQLZ?" (HOW to Get a GOUD EJUKAASHUN without Robbing the Bank!) By The Worldwide People's Revolution!® Book 020B. (This Inspired Book contains the New MAGNIFIED Version {NMV} of *First Corinthians 13*, plus: HOW to Produce Pure Living Water!)

[_] 40-021 — "The LUSCIOUS All-Mineral Organic Method of Gardening!" (HOW to Grow DELICIOUS Satisfying Foods for Potential Kingz and Kweenz in Beautiful Swanky PALACES!) By The Worldwide People's Revolution!® Book 021B. (This Book Explains HOW to make a Flood-proof Garden, while Trapping the Rainwater.)

[_] 40-022 — "Did God or Satan Ordain Medical Doctors?" (Ask Huck Finn and/or Nigger Jim: because neither Tom Sawyer nor Judge Thatcher would Know!) By The Worldwide People's Revolution!® Book 022B. (This Inspired Book Reveals HOW to Prevent Common Colds, and has a Special Chapter that Explains what a True "Nigger" IS. Surprise yourself!)

[_] 40-023 — "The BIG White OUTHOUSE on the Not-so-Biblical Capitol DUNGHILL!" (The Chief Sins of the Divided States of United Lies!) By The Worldwide People's Revolution!® Book 023B. (This Book contains Special Words that most People have never Heard! Surprise yourself again!)

[_] 40-024 — "The Public School of IGNERUNT FQLZ!" (HOW we have been GRAATLEE DISEEVD by Capitalism!) By The Worldwide People's Revolution!® Book 024B. (This Book Teaches Children HOW to "Reed and Riit in Funetik Ingglish in just wun Daa!" You should Challenge your Frendz and Naaberz with it.)

[_] 40-025 — "In thu Beeginingz uv Thingz!" (Thu Kreeaashun Stooree frum thu Beegining!) By The Worldwide People's Revolution!® Book 025B. {The Original Cover Photo showed a Picture of a Golden Supootaa (Sapote), which not one Person in a Million has ever Tasted: because it does not Ship very well, in spite of it being one of the most Sweetest Pleasant Fruits known to Mankind, which must Ripen on the Tree to be Extremely Good, after it is Grown Properly by "The LUSCIOUS All-Mineral Organic Method of Gardening!" Book 021B, which Means that the Topsoil must have all of the Proper Minerals in it. Remember the Grapes of Eschol, which the Children of Israel brought back from the Promised Land in the *Book of Joshua,* which Required 2 Strong Men to Carry just one Cluster! See the Fascinating Photos in: "Orgimmick Gardening at its Best!" (HOW to Grow Delicious Satisfying Foods without a 10 Million-Dollar Investment!) By The Worldwide People's Revolution!® Book 079.}

[_] 40-026 — "God Speaks and the Whole World Listens!" (Fire on the Mountain from the Burning Bush by the Spirit of Truths!) By The Worldwide People's Revolution!® Book 026B. (This Powerful Book contains the Best Noah Story of all of the Books, including that of Gilgamesh the Great of Ancient Babylon!)

[_] 40-027 — "Does a Good Soldier have to be a MURDERER?" (Seven Great Swanky Armies of Voluntary Working Soldiers!) By

The Worldwide People's Revolution!® Book 027B. (Chapter 03 contains a True-Life Story about a Dog Pile, which happened to the Author when he was just 10 Years Old.)

[ ] 40-028 — "Thu Nq MAGNUFIID Verzhun uv Thu PROVERBZ uv KING SOLUMUN in Plaan Ingglish!" (The Understandable Version of the Famous Proverbs of King Solomon in Plain English!) By The Worldwide People's Revolution!® Book 028. (This Marvelous Book MAGNIFIES each Proverb unto the Glory of the Great God of Inspiration, which is taken from the Original 4,000-page Book, which was written in less than 2 Months by the GIFT of Inspiration, which also contains the Famous Proverbs of Queen Izubelu!)

[ ] 40-029 — "Unlimited Enerjee 99 Percent Pollutions Free!" (HOW to Obtain FREE ElecTrickery, Worldwide!) By The Worldwide People's Revolution!® Book 029. (This Book contains the Jackson Brower Suicide, among many other Fascinating Subjects.) The Updated Version is called: "UNLIMITED ENERGY 99 Percent Pollution-Free!" (HOW to Obtain Free ElecTrickery, Worldwide!) By The Worldwide People's Revolution!® Book 029B.

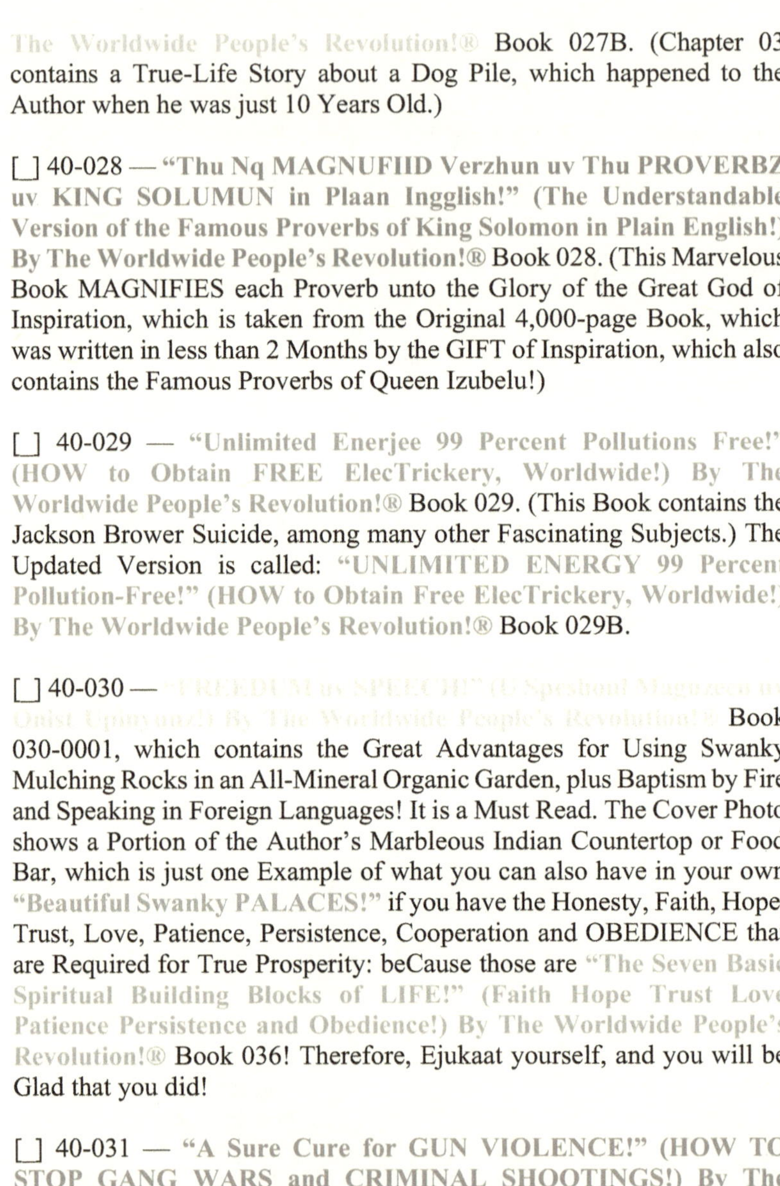

[ ] 40-030 — "FREEDUM uv SPEECH!" (U Speshool Magazeen uv Onist Upinyunz!) By The Worldwide People's Revolution!® Book 030-0001, which contains the Great Advantages for Using Swanky Mulching Rocks in an All-Mineral Organic Garden, plus Baptism by Fire and Speaking in Foreign Languages! It is a Must Read. The Cover Photo shows a Portion of the Author's Marbleous Indian Countertop or Food Bar, which is just one Example of what you can also have in your own "Beautiful Swanky PALACES!" if you have the Honesty, Faith, Hope, Trust, Love, Patience, Persistence, Cooperation and OBEDIENCE that are Required for True Prosperity: beCause those are "The Seven Basic Spiritual Building Blocks of LIFE!" (Faith Hope Trust Love Patience Persistence and Obedience!) By The Worldwide People's Revolution!® Book 036! Therefore, Ejukaat yourself, and you will be Glad that you did!

[ ] 40-031 — "A Sure Cure for GUN VIOLENCE!" (HOW TO STOP GANG WARS and CRIMINAL SHOOTINGS!) By The Worldwide People's Revolution!® Book 031. {The Cover Photo shows a Picture of a Short Shotgun, which is Fully Loaded with Double 00 Shells, and is Ready for any Tax Master who might Attempt to Steal the Retirement Home, who never moved a Finger to Help Build the Rock Houses, whereby we moved more than 66,666,666 Pounds by Hand,

whose Property was Cunningly Stolen by that False Anti-Christ WICKED Cover-up Government, which allowed Bankers to Rob us of 30 Years of Hard Labor and more than 300,000 dollars-worth of Investments in our Uncommon American Farm, which is Explained in: "LIGHTNING STRIKES Versus Lightning Bugs!" (HOW you can Become Moderately RICH, without Telling any Lies nor Selling any Trash!) By The Worldwide People's Revolution!® Book 074, which contains many Photographs with Profound Explanations! Do not be left out in the Darkness of Ignorance. Get Informed, now: beCause, **"The Great False Economy is now DEBUNKED!"** Book 053.}

[_] 40-032 — "AIIRMWVC and Reasonable Solutions!" (Aliens, Illegal Immigrants, Refugees, Migrant Workers and other Victims of Capitalism!) By The Worldwide People's Revolution!® Book 032. (This Inspired Book contains *the New MAGNIFIED Version of Job 33*.)

[_] 40-033 — "MARK TWAIN Races for the PRESIDENCY with a Landslide VICTORY!" (The 2020 Presidential Candidates Desperately Need Some STRONG Undefeatable COMPETITION!) By The Worldwide People's Revolution!® Book 033B. {This Book contains a Part of the Author's Autobiography, and his Personal Answers to the Questions in: "The Complete SURVEYS of our VALUES!" (SURVEYS of Religious Spiritual Political Governmental Sexual Social Moral Economic Business Labor Habitual and Miscellaneous VALUES!) Book 059. **The CONDENSED Version** is Book 033C, which most People Prefer.}

[_] 40-034 — "ECCLESIASTES Uncovered and Recovered!" (The New MAGNIFIED Version of Ecclesiastes and the Song of Solomon in Plain English!) By The Worldwide People's Revolution!® Book 034. (This is the Book that contains the Famous Sayings for *"There is a Time to be Born, and a Time to Die ..."* which has been Greatly Magnified!)

[_] 40-035 — "The Environmentalists' Perfect Paradise!" (HOW almost Everyone can be Living in a Beautiful Manmade Paradise!) By The Worldwide People's Revolution!® Book 035C. (This Book contains the NMV of *Psalm 48,* which will Amaze you, O Lady Doubtfulness!)

[_] 40-036 — "The Seven Basic Spiritual Building Blocks of LIFE!" (Faith Hope Trust Love Patience Persistence and Obedience!) By The Worldwide People's Revolution!® Book 036. (This Book contains the Mockingbird's Version of *Hebrews 11,* plus the NMV of *First Corinthians 13,* among many other "Goodies.")

[_] 40-037 — "DIETS!" (A Reasonable Solution for the "Eternal Controversy"!) By The Worldwide People's Revolution!® Book 037.

[_] 40-038 — "The Nature of CAPITALISM!" (A List of the EVILS of CAPITALISM!) By The Worldwide People's Revolution!® Book 038.

[_] 40-039 — "SWANGKEENOMIKS Rules the Roost!" (HOW all People can Prosper in a RIIT WAA, and STOP Polluting the Earth with Capitalist TRASH!) By The Worldwide People's Revolution!® Book 039. (The Cover Photo shows a Portion of the Author's Retirement Home, before the 5,000+ square-feet Concrete Roof was Installed, after moving more than 66 Million Pounds by Hand, and mostly by his own Boastful Hands!)

[_] 40-040 — "The New MAGNIFIED Version of The Book of MORMON!" (The Story of the White and Dark Indians in the Americas!) By Big Chief Standsover Bull in River of Life! Book 040, which comes in 2 Volumes of about 500 Pages, each. The Cover Photo on the First Volume shows the Queen of England's Golden Coach, and the Cover Photo on the Second Volume shows one of many Polished Spanish Marble Walls in our Selected King's Retirement Home, which is worth a thousand dollars per square yard, which is another Example of what you can also have, if you simply OBEY your Righteous KING! All such Marble is very Inspiring. No one could Study it for very long without Believing in a Great Creator God. The Picture does not do it Justice. You would have to See it in Person, and Wash it with Pure Water to bring Out the Beauty of it.

[_] 40-041 — "The GREAT Worldwide TELEVISED Court HEARING!" (That Great Meeting of the Most-Intelligent and Well-Educated Minds!) By The Worldwide People's Revolution!® Book 041B. {This is the Book that the World has long been Waiting for: beCause it will Overthrow the Evil Empires, and make it Possible to Establish "The New RIGHTEOUS One-World Government!" (HOW to Establish a Righteous One-World Government without Going to WAR!) By The Worldwide People's Revolution!® Book 056. This is the Greatest Idea since the Invention of the Light Bulb, Guaranteed!}

[_] 40-042 — "The Secret City of the Great King!" (HOW the True Church will Escape from the Great Tribulation!) By The Worldwide People's Revolution!® Book 042. (Be Sure to Inform your Friends, Relatives and Naaberz about this Wonderful Book: beCause they might also Want to Escape!)

[_] 40-043 — "Terrorists Beware that your Days are Numbered!" (HOW to Bring those Terrorist Attacks to a Screeching HALT!) By The Worldwide People's Revolution!® Book 043. (This Book also contains the Fascinating Book of LEHI, which has now been Restored!) †‡

[_] 40-044 — "The New MAGNIFIED Version of ISAIAH in Plain English!" (The Understandable Version of the Book of Isaiah!) By The Worldwide People's Revolution!® Book 044. (The Cover Photo shows a Swanky Potato and Avocado Salad with Sweet Peas and Corn, among other "Secret" Ingredients, which are Revealed within the Book. Remember that you can read many Words for Free in the Book Previews on www.Amazon.com.usa or UK.)

[_] 40-045 — "HOW to Become a HOLY Man!" (40 Good Reasons WHY People Should FAST and PRAY!) By The Worldwide People's Revolution!® Book 045, which is a Companion Book of:

[_] 40-046 — "The Proper RULES for FASTING!" (The Complete Instruction Manual for True Repentance!) By The Worldwide People's Revolution!® Book 046, which is a Companion Book of the above-mentioned Book, which contains a True-Life Story about an Old Black Mare called Lucy, who Fasted for 30 Days without Food nor Water, who was Physiologically "Born Again," as Jesus might say. See the Full Details in: "The New MAGNIFIED Version of The GOOD NEWS According to Saint JOHN!" (The Gospel According to Saint John Zebedee Boanerges in Plain English!) Book 062, which contains many Inspiring Photographs with Explanations!

[_] 40-047 — "Are Americans the Most-STUPID People who ever Lived?" (HOW Working People can PROSPER and Live in PEACE Under the Rulership of a RIGHTEOUS KING!) By The Worldwide People's Revolution!® Book 047. (The Cover Photo shows a large Portion of the Author's Living Room Floor, which is worth 100,000$, which is just another Good Example of what you can also have, just for Loving and Obeying your Elected King!)

[_] 40-048 — "An Amazing Collection of Wit and Wisdom!" (The Marvelous Tale of the Colorful Peacock from Angel Ridge, and the Strong Rope of Everlasting Hope!) By The Worldwide People's Revolution!® Book 048. (The Cover Photo shows a Book Display, which will be Greatly Enhanced during the Future, when all 364+ Inspired Books are on Display in a Swanky Truth-brary, as Opposed to the Public LIE-brary.)

[_] 40-049 — "Justifications for Capitalizations!" (WHY our Selected King DEFIES the School of FOOLS by Capitalizing LOVE and HATE!) By The Worldwide People's Revolution!® Book 049.

[_] 40-050 — "The END of CONFUSION!" (The Great CELEBRATION of the Magnificent Wedding of the Most-Humble, Honest Nations, and the Grand Year of JUBILEE!) By The Worldwide People's Revolution!® Book 050. (Just Try to Visualize those **"Seven Great Swanky Armies of Voluntary Working Soldiers"** Marching through the Valley of Megiddo, being Dressed in their Colorful Robes, while the Band Plays *The Battle Hymn of the Republic,* and the Choirs Sing the Praises of the Great KING of Kings! What a Sight and Sound that will be, which will be Climaxed in "The Great World TEMPLE of PEACE," when the Nations will get Married, along with our Elected King! Come one, come all to "The GREAT Worldwide TELEVISED Court HEARING," by Means of your Wide Flat-screen TVs, whereby you might Learn WHY, WHEN and HOW!) †‡

[_] 40-051 — "The Loathsome Burdens of the Independent Jackasses!" (A New Civilized Approach for Quietly Solving our Massive Problems!) By The Worldwide People's Revolution!® Book 051. (Just Think about the Multitude of almost Worthless Meetings of the Minds, who Strained themselves to Think of Reasonable Solutions for our Massive Problems, who sometimes even Prayed to God for Help; but, the Best Solutions have been here for no less than 40 Years — Thanks to the Spirit of Inspiration from GOD!)

[_] 40-052 — "Are we Tax Slaves of a Lower Order than those Lying Conniving EDOMITES!" (HOW to be Liberated From all Forms of Slavery, Worldwide!) By The Worldwide People's Revolution!® Book 052B. {This Inspired Book once had another Title and Author, which was not Acceptable by Amazon, which has now been Restored in all of its Glory, and is Published by more Trustworthy People, who are not Afraid of Controversies, nor of: "The Swanky Sword of Divine

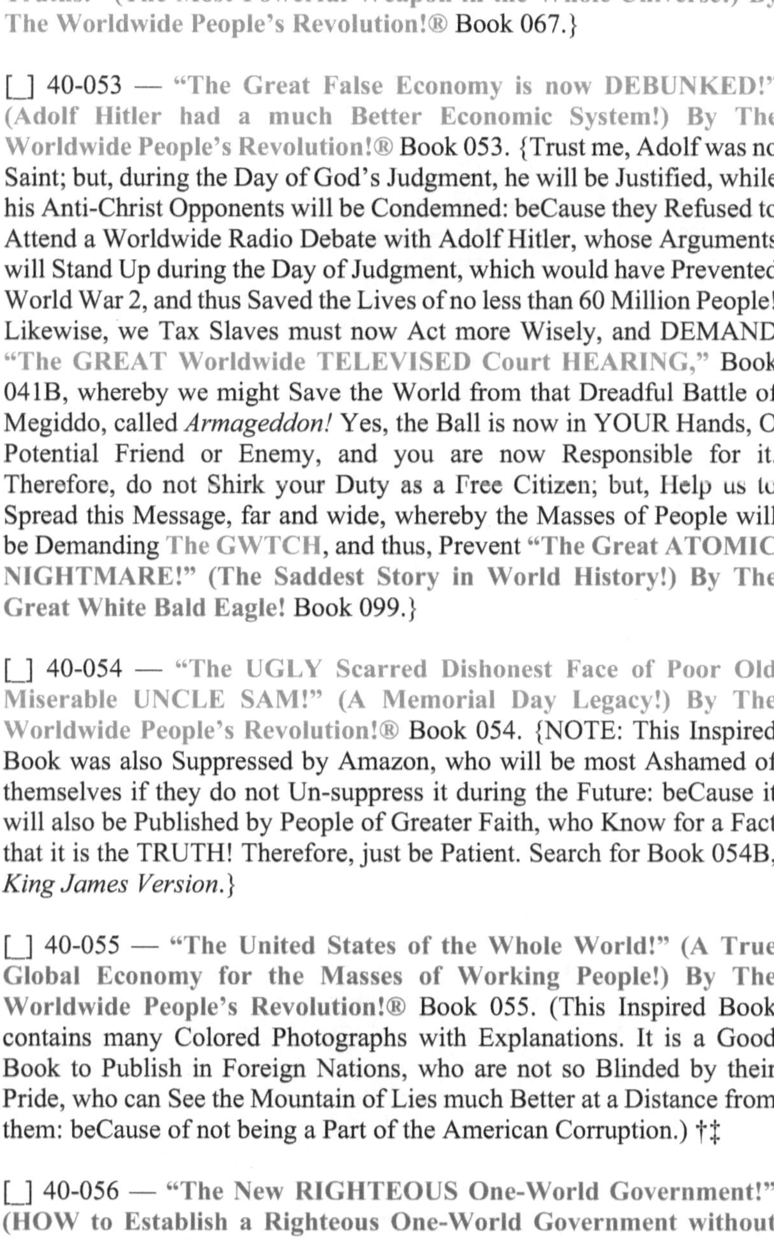

Truths!" (The Most-Powerful Weapon in the Whole Universe!) By The Worldwide People's Revolution!® Book 067.}

[_] 40-053 — "The Great False Economy is now DEBUNKED!" (Adolf Hitler had a much Better Economic System!) By The Worldwide People's Revolution!® Book 053. {Trust me, Adolf was no Saint; but, during the Day of God's Judgment, he will be Justified, while his Anti-Christ Opponents will be Condemned: beCause they Refused to Attend a Worldwide Radio Debate with Adolf Hitler, whose Arguments will Stand Up during the Day of Judgment, which would have Prevented World War 2, and thus Saved the Lives of no less than 60 Million People! Likewise, we Tax Slaves must now Act more Wisely, and DEMAND "The GREAT Worldwide TELEVISED Court HEARING," Book 041B, whereby we might Save the World from that Dreadful Battle of Megiddo, called *Armageddon!* Yes, the Ball is now in YOUR Hands, O Potential Friend or Enemy, and you are now Responsible for it. Therefore, do not Shirk your Duty as a Free Citizen; but, Help us to Spread this Message, far and wide, whereby the Masses of People will be Demanding The GWTCH, and thus, Prevent "The Great ATOMIC NIGHTMARE!" (The Saddest Story in World History!) By The Great White Bald Eagle! Book 099.}

[_] 40-054 — "The UGLY Scarred Dishonest Face of Poor Old Miserable UNCLE SAM!" (A Memorial Day Legacy!) By The Worldwide People's Revolution!® Book 054. {NOTE: This Inspired Book was also Suppressed by Amazon, who will be most Ashamed of themselves if they do not Un-suppress it during the Future: beCause it will also be Published by People of Greater Faith, who Know for a Fact that it is the TRUTH! Therefore, just be Patient. Search for Book 054B, *King James Version.*}

[_] 40-055 — "The United States of the Whole World!" (A True Global Economy for the Masses of Working People!) By The Worldwide People's Revolution!® Book 055. (This Inspired Book contains many Colored Photographs with Explanations. It is a Good Book to Publish in Foreign Nations, who are not so Blinded by their Pride, who can See the Mountain of Lies much Better at a Distance from them: beCause of not being a Part of the American Corruption.) †‡

[_] 40-056 — "The New RIGHTEOUS One-World Government!" (HOW to Establish a Righteous One-World Government without Going to WAR!) By The Worldwide People's Revolution!® Book

056. (This is a KEY Book, which everyone should Study Carefully and Prayerfully.)

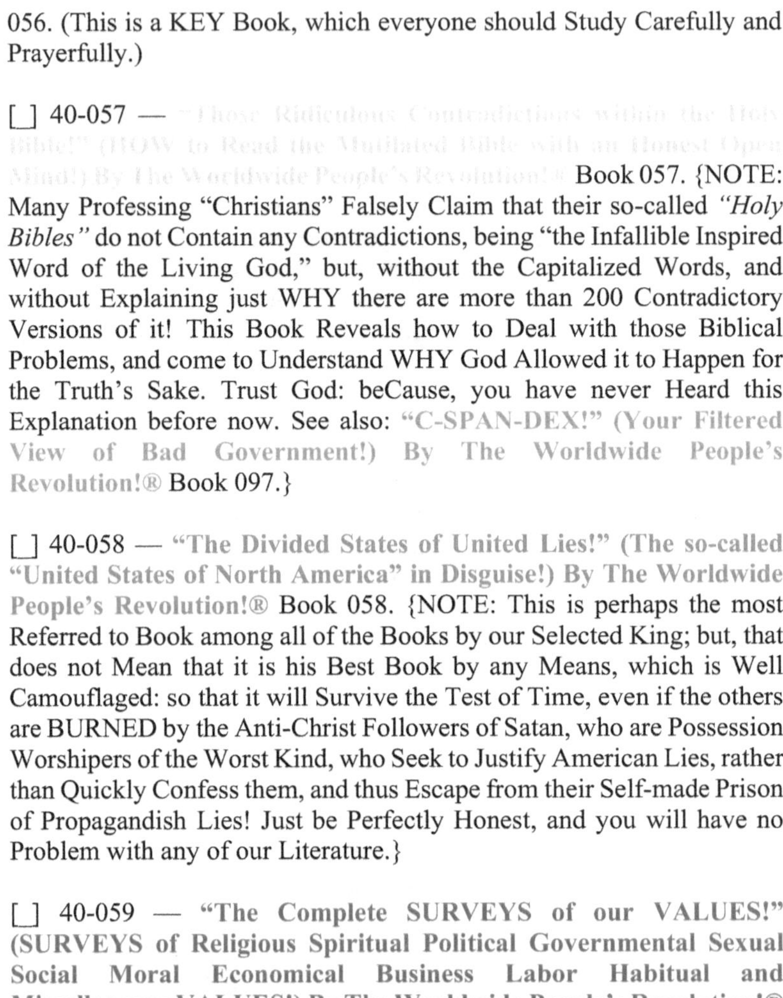

[_] 40-057 — "Those Ridiculous Contradictions within the Holy Bible!" (HOW to Read the Mutilated Bible with an Honest Open Mind!) By The Worldwide People's Revolution!® Book 057. {NOTE: Many Professing "Christians" Falsely Claim that their so-called *"Holy Bibles"* do not Contain any Contradictions, being "the Infallible Inspired Word of the Living God," but, without the Capitalized Words, and without Explaining just WHY there are more than 200 Contradictory Versions of it! This Book Reveals how to Deal with those Biblical Problems, and come to Understand WHY God Allowed it to Happen for the Truth's Sake. Trust God: beCause, you have never Heard this Explanation before now. See also: "C-SPAN-DEX!" (Your Filtered View of Bad Government!) By The Worldwide People's Revolution!® Book 097.}

[_] 40-058 — "The Divided States of United Lies!" (The so-called "United States of North America" in Disguise!) By The Worldwide People's Revolution!® Book 058. {NOTE: This is perhaps the most Referred to Book among all of the Books by our Selected King; but, that does not Mean that it is his Best Book by any Means, which is Well Camouflaged: so that it will Survive the Test of Time, even if the others are BURNED by the Anti-Christ Followers of Satan, who are Possession Worshipers of the Worst Kind, who Seek to Justify American Lies, rather than Quickly Confess them, and thus Escape from their Self-made Prison of Propagandish Lies! Just be Perfectly Honest, and you will have no Problem with any of our Literature.}

[_] 40-059 — "The Complete SURVEYS of our VALUES!" (SURVEYS of Religious Spiritual Political Governmental Sexual Social Moral Economical Business Labor Habitual and Miscellaneous VALUES!) By The Worldwide People's Revolution!® Book 059. {NOTE: According to our Selected King, every Potential Leader in the World must Fill Out and File those Surveys on the Internet for everyone to Study, whereby the Best People might be Elected by those Wise People who have also Filled Out the Simplistic Surveys of their own Values, whereby they will be Qualified to VOTE. Otherwise, they will not be Qualified to Vote, which will Eliminate a LOT of Wasted Money on Election Deceptions, while at the same Time it will Educate a lot of Ignorant People, who Desperately Need to Study that Inspired Book before Voting for another Dimwitcrat, Reprobate, or Independent Jackass!}

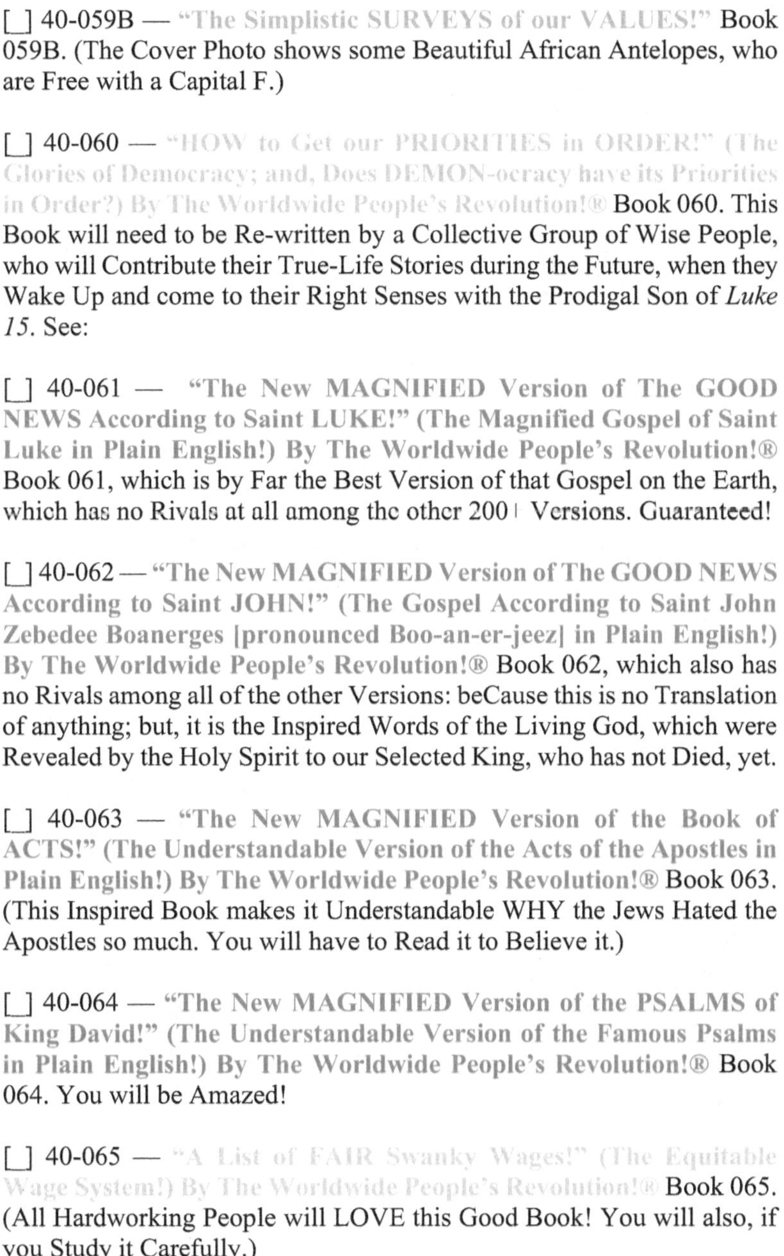

[_] 40-059B — "The Simplistic SURVEYS of our VALUES!" Book 059B. (The Cover Photo shows some Beautiful African Antelopes, who are Free with a Capital F.)

[_] 40-060 — "HOW to Get our PRIORITIES in ORDER!" (The Glories of Democracy; and, Does DEMON-ocracy have its Priorities in Order?) By The Worldwide People's Revolution!® Book 060. This Book will need to be Re-written by a Collective Group of Wise People, who will Contribute their True-Life Stories during the Future, when they Wake Up and come to their Right Senses with the Prodigal Son of *Luke 15*. See:

[_] 40-061 — "The New MAGNIFIED Version of The GOOD NEWS According to Saint LUKE!" (The Magnified Gospel of Saint Luke in Plain English!) By The Worldwide People's Revolution!® Book 061, which is by Far the Best Version of that Gospel on the Earth, which has no Rivals at all among the other 200 ı Versions. Guaranteed!

[_] 40-062 — "The New MAGNIFIED Version of The GOOD NEWS According to Saint JOHN!" (The Gospel According to Saint John Zebedee Boanerges [pronounced Boo-an-er-jeez] in Plain English!) By The Worldwide People's Revolution!® Book 062, which also has no Rivals among all of the other Versions: beCause this is no Translation of anything; but, it is the Inspired Words of the Living God, which were Revealed by the Holy Spirit to our Selected King, who has not Died, yet.

[_] 40-063 — "The New MAGNIFIED Version of the Book of ACTS!" (The Understandable Version of the Acts of the Apostles in Plain English!) By The Worldwide People's Revolution!® Book 063. (This Inspired Book makes it Understandable WHY the Jews Hated the Apostles so much. You will have to Read it to Believe it.)

[_] 40-064 — "The New MAGNIFIED Version of the PSALMS of King David!" (The Understandable Version of the Famous Psalms in Plain English!) By The Worldwide People's Revolution!® Book 064. You will be Amazed!

[_] 40-065 — "A List of FAIR Swanky Wages!" (The Equitable Wage System!) By The Worldwide People's Revolution!® Book 065. (All Hardworking People will LOVE this Good Book! You will also, if you Study it Carefully.)

[_] 40-066 — "Beautiful Swanky PALACES!" (A New Concept in Living Habits — Swanky Palaces for Poor People!) By The Worldwide People's Revolution!® Book 066. (You have no Idea what a "Swanky Palace" IS, unless you have read this Unique Book, or another one that Describes those Palaces, and several of them do; but, this one has the Best Description. ENJOY!)

[_] 40-067 — "The Swanky Sword of Divine Truths!" (The Most-Powerful Weapon in the Whole Universe!) By The Worldwide People's Revolution!® Book 067. (The very Reason that our Selected King has no Rivals is beCause of the Swanky Sword of Divine Truths, which no one can Defeat by any Means. Therefore, you Need to have it on your own Side, whereby no one can Defeat your Arguments! Be Strong, be Brave, have Faith and put on the Whole Armor of GOD!)

[_] 40-068 — "Has your Life become Extremely Complicated?" (HOW to Live a SIMPLE Life!) By The Worldwide People's Revolution!® Book 068. (Many People are not even Aware of just how Complicated their Lives are, until suddenly they are ready to Commit Suicide! It is Best to Prevent all such Evil Things, and this Book tells HOW.)

[_] 40-069 — "The IDEAL Place to Live!" (HOW to Discover the Ideal Place to Live!) By The Worldwide People's Revolution!® Book 069. {NOTE: Our Selected King Searched the World over, and did not Discover any Idea Place to Live. Therefore, he Concluded that we must Make our own. Yes, we must Build those "GLORIOUS Swanky Hotels Castles and Fortresses!" (Beautiful Planned City States for WISE Intelligent Well-Educated People with Common Sense and Good Understanding!) By The Worldwide People's Revolution!® Book 019B, even if we must DRAFT "Seven Great Armies of Working Soldiers!" (HOW to Provide a Way for Everyone to WORK: so as to Eliminate Poverty, Crimes, Drug Abuses, Prisons and Unnecessary Taxes!) By The Worldwide People's Revolution!® Book 015B; and what on this Good Earth could Prove to be more Profitable than that, and without going to WAR?}

[_] 40-070 — "Our Elected King Who Speaks Out!" (It is High Time for some Sane Person to Get Control of this Insane World!) By The Worldwide People's Revolution!® Book 070. (This Inspired Book contains a Special Speech that is Addressed to both Houses of the Congress in Washington. You will Love it, O Honest Man of Greater Faith!)

[_] 40-071 — "How GAY is GOD?" (Oh, the Wonders of it all, when it ALL Hangs Out!) By The Worldwide People's Revolution!® Book 071. (Do not Judge the Book, until you have Carefully "Red" all of it. You will be Surprised by the Provable Truths within it, and Greatly Humored by the Author's Exceptionally Good Humor, who is less Gay than God, who has never had any Sexual Intercourse during his entire Life! In other Words, he is a VIRGIN!)

[_] 40-072 — "LIGHTNING STRIKES Versus Lightning Bugs and Impotent Fireflies!" (A Memorial Photo Album of some Real American Heroes!) By The Worldwide People's Revolution!® Book 072. (NOTE: This Book is Unique among all of the Books by our Selected King: beCause he did not get to Proof-read it before the Computer Crashed. It just Happened to be Saved on a Computer Chip before the Computer Crashed, and therefore it was Saved in PDF. But, the Corrections did not get made, which makes it a Special Collector's Item, which has more than 100 Colored Photos, which was what Caused the Crash.) †‡

[_] 40-073 — "The BEST of CAPITALISM!" (Corrections for: "LIGHTNING STRIKES Versus Lightning Bugs and Impotent Fireflies!") Book 073. (It is a completely new Book, except for those Corrections; and it is one of the Best Books in the World, which all Honest People will Love.)

[_] 40-074 — "LIGHTNING STRIKES Versus Lightning Bugs!" (HOW you can Become Moderately RICH, without Telling any Lies nor Selling any Trash!) By The Worldwide People's Revolution!® Book 074, which is the Perfection of all of the Lightning Striking Books, which is Recommended above all others for Mass Production: beCause it stands the Best Chance of being a Real Winner, just after this Book that you are now Reading, which has a Magnetizing Title!

[_] 40-075 — "What are the PUNISHMENTS for Dietary Sins?" (Have we Served ourselves Well at the Tables of our Lusts?) By The Worldwide People's Revolution!® Book 075. (This Book is too Controversial to be Published at this Time. Be very Patient until it is Available: beCause it is HOT!)

[_] 40-076 — "What is WRong with those CRAZY CHRISTIANS?" (A Self-Examination of the Heart of the Body of Good Government!) By The Worldwide People's Revolution!® Book 076.

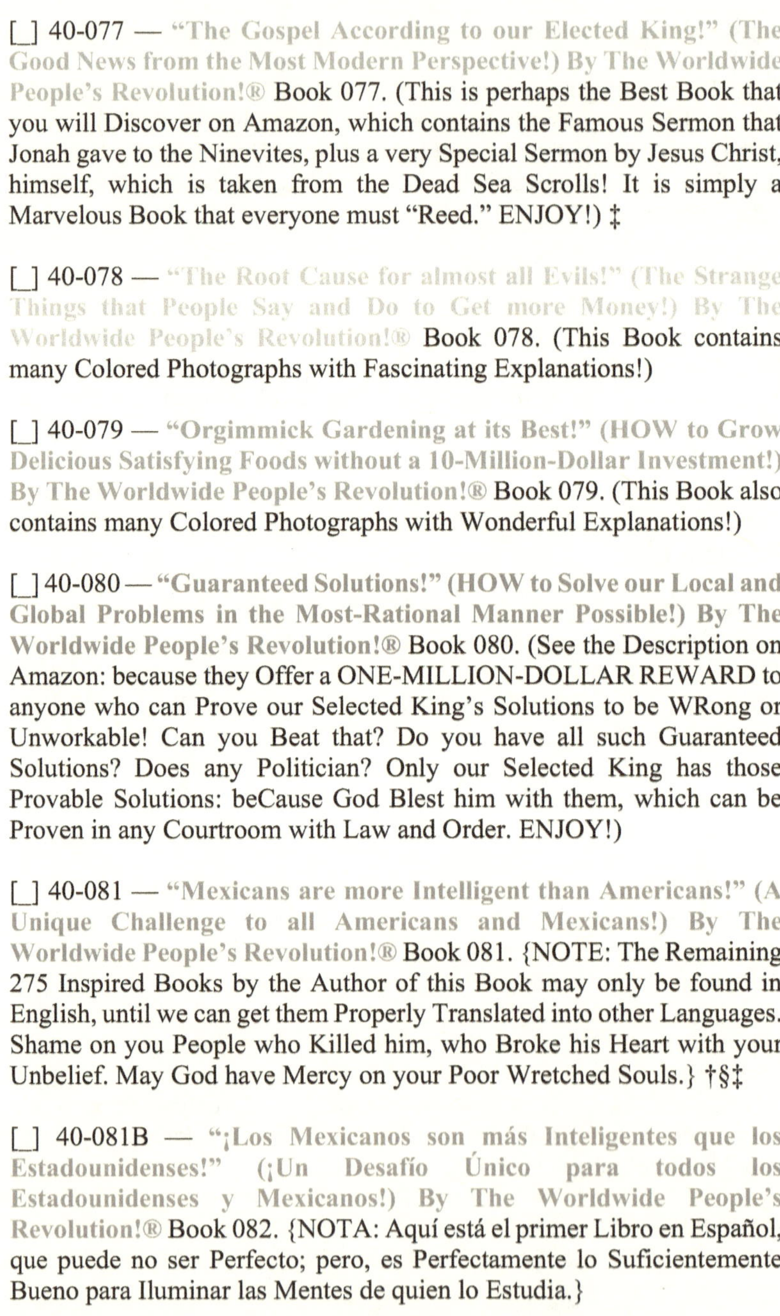

[_] 40-077 — "The Gospel According to our Elected King!" (The Good News from the Most Modern Perspective!) By The Worldwide People's Revolution!® Book 077. (This is perhaps the Best Book that you will Discover on Amazon, which contains the Famous Sermon that Jonah gave to the Ninevites, plus a very Special Sermon by Jesus Christ, himself, which is taken from the Dead Sea Scrolls! It is simply a Marvelous Book that everyone must "Reed." ENJOY!) ‡

[_] 40-078 — "The Root Cause for almost all Evils!" (The Strange Things that People Say and Do to Get more Money!) By The Worldwide People's Revolution!® Book 078. (This Book contains many Colored Photographs with Fascinating Explanations!)

[_] 40-079 — "Orgimmick Gardening at its Best!" (HOW to Grow Delicious Satisfying Foods without a 10-Million-Dollar Investment!) By The Worldwide People's Revolution!® Book 079. (This Book also contains many Colored Photographs with Wonderful Explanations!)

[_] 40-080 — "Guaranteed Solutions!" (HOW to Solve our Local and Global Problems in the Most-Rational Manner Possible!) By The Worldwide People's Revolution!® Book 080. (See the Description on Amazon: because they Offer a ONE-MILLION-DOLLAR REWARD to anyone who can Prove our Selected King's Solutions to be WRong or Unworkable! Can you Beat that? Do you have all such Guaranteed Solutions? Does any Politician? Only our Selected King has those Provable Solutions: beCause God Blest him with them, which can be Proven in any Courtroom with Law and Order. ENJOY!)

[_] 40-081 — "Mexicans are more Intelligent than Americans!" (A Unique Challenge to all Americans and Mexicans!) By The Worldwide People's Revolution!® Book 081. {NOTE: The Remaining 275 Inspired Books by the Author of this Book may only be found in English, until we can get them Properly Translated into other Languages. Shame on you People who Killed him, who Broke his Heart with your Unbelief. May God have Mercy on your Poor Wretched Souls.} †§‡

[_] 40-081B — "¡Los Mexicanos son más Inteligentes que los Estadounidenses!" (¡Un Desafío Único para todos los Estadounidenses y Mexicanos!) By The Worldwide People's Revolution!® Book 082. {NOTA: Aquí está el primer Libro en Español, que puede no ser Perfecto; pero, es Perfectamente lo Suficientemente Bueno para Iluminar las Mentes de quien lo Estudia.}

[_] 40-082 — "The Process of Making a RIGHTEOUS KING!" (A Fascinating Autobiography of our Selected King!) By The Worldwide People's Revolution!® Book 082. {NOTE: He once had a 6,000-plus-page Autobiography, called: **"DIARRHEA of the Mind!"** which gave Details of his entire Life, since he was only 4 Years Old, when he had an Encounter with God, which has been Lost: beCause those Backup Disks became Obsolete, and were thus Trashed, along with the Obsolete Computer, which Costed 4,000-plus Dollars, along with the Hewlett-Packard Printer, which Costed another 4,000-plus Dollars, whose Antiquated Software would not Work with a Modern Computer, nor did Hewlett have an Updated Software Program for it: beCause they are Capitalist Scammers, who should be put Out of Business for Practicing Donald Trump Tactics! See: "The Nature of CAPITALISM!" (A List of the EVILS of CAPITALISM!) By The Worldwide People's Revolution!® Book 038.}

[_] 40-083 — "Was Billy Graham Greatly Deceived?" (Giving Honor to whom Honor is Due!) By The Worldwide People's Revolution!® Book 083. {NOTE: If you know a Grahamite, please Direct him or her to this Inspired Book, whereby he or she might be Converted to the Truths within it, and thus be Saved from Grahamite Perversions. Thank you in Advance. They will also Thank you for it: beCause they Suffer so Needlessly, when they should be Free, Healthy and Happy, like our Selected King, who has no Aches nor Pains, who used to Work Hard all Day long, and not be Weary, just like you can Reed in *the Book of Isaiah 40:31, NMV!*}

[_] 40-084 — "The New MAGNIFIED Version of the Book of DEUTERONOMY!" (The Understandable Version of Deuteronomy in Plain English!) Book 084. This is actually one of the Best Books within the entire Holy Bible, and also one of the Longest; but, do not allow that Fact to Deter you by any Means: beCause, "the Bigger Book is Normally a Better Book," which is True of a lot of Books, including all of the above Books: beCause it is the Nature of the Holy Spirit to get into Long-winded Sermons, you might say, which is WHY the Apostle Paul Preached until Midnight in *the Book of Acts,* until some Boy went to Sleep and Fell from a Window and Killed himself, whom the Apostle Paul Raised Up from the Dead and went on Preaching until the Dawn of the Day! And it is NOT Jewish Mythology! †§‡§§ {See: "The New MAGNIFIED Version of the Book of ACTS" for the Finest of Details, Book 063.}

[_] 40-085 — "All of the Arguments are in Favor of our Selected King, who has Zero Challengers!" (Before you Attend another Election Deception, you should Carefully Study this Inspired Book with an Honest Open Mind!) By The Worldwide People's Revolution!® Book 085.

[_] 40-086 — "Provable Truths that True Christians cannot Rightly Deny!" (A Fair Challenge for all Professing "Christians" to Meditate on with Honest Open Minds!) By The Worldwide People's Revolution!® Book 086.

[_] 40-087 — "How all Women can Get True Justice without Getting Divorced from God!" (The Unjust Case of Judge Brett Kavanaugh and Doctor Christine Blasey Ford is now Revisited by a Wise Son of King Solomon!) By The Worldwide People's Revolution!® B-087.

[_] 40-088 — "The New MAGNIFIED Version of GENESIS!" (The Enlightening Version of the Beginnings of Things!) By The Worldwide People's Revolution!® Book 088.

[_] 40-089 — "The New MAGNIFIED Version of the HOLY KORAN!" (WHY MuhamMAD went to Hell for Spiritual MURDER!) By The Worldwide People's Revolution!® Book 089. This is by Far the Best Version of the *Holy Koran,* which is Loved by all Honest Muslims, Hindus, Christians and Buddhists, Worldwide! Surprise yourself and others. Ask them what it Means? §‡

[_] 40-090 — "A New Jerusalem in the Great State of Flexible Texas!" (HOW to make Good Use of the Mississippi River!) By The Worldwide People's Revolution!® Book 090. This Book contains many Fascinating Photos of God's Handiwork. ENJOY!

[_] 40-091 — "What is The GREATEST SIN?" (And it is NOT Blasphemy Against the Holy Spirit!) By The Worldwide People's Revolution!® Book 091.

[_] 40-092 — "HOW to Make America (and all other Nations) Really GREAT Without Telling any LIES!" (The Founding Fathers would have Loved it!) By The Worldwide People's Revolution!® Book 092.

[_] 40-093 — "HOW Righteousness can Overcome Wickedness!" (The Triumph of the Soul who Knows God!) By The Enlightened Professor of Common Sense! Book 093. {Notice how the Calves in the

Cover Photo Segregated themselves by their Colors, from Left to Right. God Guided them. ‡}

[_] 40-094 — "Justifications for MAGNIFICATIONS!" (The Problem with Understanding a Complicated Contradictory Mutilated Unholy Bible!) Or: (The Problem with Inventing Lies that are too BIG to DIE!) By The Worldwide People's Revolution!® Book 094.

[_] 40-095 — "HOW to IDENTIFY God's Elected Ones!" (Are YOU one of the Elect?) By The Worldwide People's Revolution!® Book 095.

[_] 40-096 — "GOVERNMENT Versus Independence!" (How Much CONTROL Should a Government Have?") By The Worldwide People's Revolution!® Book 096.

[_] 40-097 — "C-SPAN-DEX!" (Your Filtered View of Bad Government!) By The Worldwide People's Revolution!® Book 097.

[_] 40-098 — "Profitable Swanky MULCHING ROCKS!" (30 Advantages for Using Swanky Mulching Rocks in an All-Mineral Organic Garden!) By The Worldwide People's Revolution!® Book 098. {Just Think, the School of Fools never Mentioned them, nor did the False Government, nor any of the False Churches: beCause they are Uneducated and Foolish.}

[_] 40-099 — "The Great ATOMIC NIGHTMARE!" (The Saddest Story in World History!) By The Great White Bald Eagle! Book 099. {NOTE: Let us Hope and Pray that no one ever has to Write this Book; but, if they Do, it should Spook the Devil Out of you!}

[_] 40-100 — "Our Selected King SPEAKS OUT!" (It is High Time for some Sane Person to get Total Control of this Insane World!) By The Worldwide People's Revolution!® Book 100!

[_] 40-101 — "What will you Do when the Rain STOPS?" (God's Last Resort to Save Mankind from his MADNESS!) By The Worldwide People's Revolution!® Book 101!

[_] 40-102 — "Beautiful Swanky Stone Dome Home COMPLEXES!" (HOW to Build SECURE Tax-proof, Insurance-proof, Self-air-conditioned, Paint-proof, Rot-proof, Termite-proof, Mouse-proof, Fireproof, Tornado-proof, Hurricane-proof, Thief-proof, and BOMB-PROOF Houses!) By The Worldwide People's Revolution!® Book 102.

[ ] 40-103 — "Royal Swanky Buffets!" (The Best Feasts in the Whole World!) By The Worldwide People's Revolution!® Book 103.

[ ] 40-104 — "101 Good Reasons and Great Advantages for Establishing a Righteous One-World Government!" (Government By the People, Of the People, and For the People!) By The Worldwide People's Revolution!® Book 104. This Book Suggests thousands of Good Reasons and Great Advantages. But, of course, you have to be Able to THINK, which seems to be something that Wicked Politicians cannot Do, or Refuse to Do; and neither can most Preachers and Teachers Do it. Therefore, this Inspired Book will Help them to Think and Remember.

[ ] 40-105 — "The New MAGNIFIED Version of the Book of REVELATION!" (The Understandable Version of the Most-Controversial Book in the Whole World!) By The Worldwide People's Revolution!® Book 105. This Proverbial "Bombshell" will be Published just before the Second Coming of Jesus Christ! Get your Seatbelts Fastened! Be Prepared for Radical Changes!

[ ] 40-106 — "The Naked Glory of Beautiful Mankind!" (1,000 Pages of Sheer Artistic BEAUTY!) By The Worldwide People's Revolution!® Book 106. (See Book 014B-02-09-T for the Explanation.)

[ ] 40-107 — "The Beautiful Faces of Holy Men!" (The very Best that God has to Offer!) By The Worldwide People's Revolution!® Book 107.

[ ] 40-108 — "The Worldwide People's Revolution!" (A Comprehensive Plan for Obtaining Worldwide Law, Order, Obedience, Peace and True Prosperity!) By The Worldwide People's Revolution!® Book 108.

[ ] 40-109 — "VOTE for The GOAT!" (The New Political Party that has Guaranteed Solutions for our Massive Problems!) By The Worldwide People's Revolution!® Book 109.

[_] 40-110 — "IMPORTANT THINGS that Should Have Been Written in the Holy Bible!" (A Special Challenge to all Professing Christians, Jews, Hindus, Muslims and Atheists!) **By The Irreverent Penname Scumbag!** Book 110.

[_] 40-111 — **"Hosts of HOAXES Live In Under Around and Over the Little White OUTHOUSE!"** (WHY Spiritually-Blind Cowardly-Americans are Hunkering Down in their Empty Root Cellars!) **By The Irreverent Penname Oversight!** Book 111.

[_] 40-112 — "Should Wives Obey their Husbands?" (OR, Should Husbands OBEY their Wives?) By The Irreverent Penname Mockingbird! Book 112.

[_] 40-113 — "Modern Deceived SLAVES!" (10 Simple Steps for Liberating ALL Modern Slaves, Worldwide, Including Yourself!) **By Liberty and Justice for ALL!** Book 113.

[_] 40-114 — "Are you a Jobless Graduate of the School of Fools?" (How to Obtain a Good Education without Robbing the Bank, Selling any Trash, nor Telling any Lies!) **By The Professor Wordcraft Enlightenment!** Book 114.

[_] 40-115 — "Beautiful Swanky FASTING SANITARIUMS!" (HOW to Learn Good Self-Discipline!) **By The Worldwide People's Revolution!®** Book 115.
[_] 40-116 — "Swanky Institutions for Compassionate Corrections!" (How to Correct even the Most-Stubborn Bullies!) **By The Biggest Bully of All Bullies!** Book 116.

[_] 40-117 — "What is True PROGRESS???" (Are we Making any True Progress, at all?) **By The Worldwide People's Revolution!®** Book 117.

[_] 40-118 — "Is America a White Nation with a Black Heart?" (How to Separate Truth from Fiction!) **By The Good Pastor of Uncommon Sense!** Book 118.

[_] 40-119 — "Which Church is the Right Church?" (Can all Churches be Correct?) **By The Good Pastor of Uncommon Sense!** Book 119.

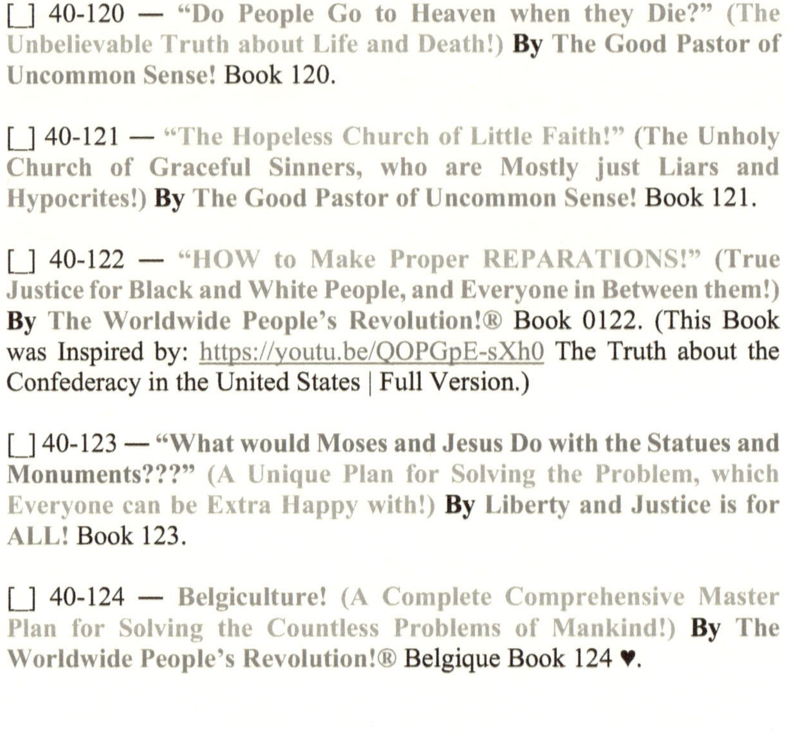

[_] 40-120 — "Do People Go to Heaven when they Die?" (The Unbelievable Truth about Life and Death!) **By The Good Pastor of Uncommon Sense!** Book 120.

[_] 40-121 — "The Hopeless Church of Little Faith!" (The Unholy Church of Graceful Sinners, who are Mostly just Liars and Hypocrites!) **By The Good Pastor of Uncommon Sense!** Book 121.

[_] 40-122 — "HOW to Make Proper REPARATIONS!" (True Justice for Black and White People, and Everyone in Between them!) **By The Worldwide People's Revolution!®** Book 0122. (This Book was Inspired by: https://youtu.be/QOPGpE-sXh0 The Truth about the Confederacy in the United States | Full Version.)

[_] 40-123 — "What would Moses and Jesus Do with the Statues and Monuments???" (A Unique Plan for Solving the Problem, which Everyone can be Extra Happy with!) **By Liberty and Justice is for ALL!** Book 123.

[_] 40-124 — Belgiculture! (A Complete Comprehensive Master Plan for Solving the Countless Problems of Mankind!) **By The Worldwide People's Revolution!®** Belgique Book 124 ♥.

{NOTE: That List of Available Books will be Updated, Periodically, if we do not get Killed by some Thugs, who Work for those Lying Conniving Edomites!}